CLOUT

a play by David Young

COACH HOUSE BOOKS

first edition

Published with the assistance of the Canada Council for the Arts and the Ontario Arts Council

NATIONAL LIBRARY OF CANADA CATALOGUING IN PUBLICATION DATA

Young, David, 1946 –
Clout

1st ed.
A play.
ISBN 1-55245-077-5

I. Title

PS8579.059C56 2001 C812'.54 C2001-930133-2
PR9199.3.Y68C56 2001

This play is dedicated to the memory of poet and painter

Roy Kiyooka, a wise and funny man.

PRODUCTION HISTORY

Clout was commissioned by the Necessary Angel Theatre Company in Toronto. The play premiered at the National Arts Centre, 26 January 2001, as a National Arts Centre/Factory Theatre/Necessary Angel co-production.

The Cast:

TRENT – Eric Peterson
EVE/RENEE/NURSE – Waneta Storms
LIONEL K. BIGGAR – R.H. Thomson

Director – Richard Rose
Set and Lighting Design – Graeme S. Thomson
Costume Design – Carolyn M. Smith
Music and Sound Design – Michael Phillip Wojewoda
Assistant Director – Isaac Meyer Odell
Stage Manager – Susan Monis
Apprentice Stage Manager – Angela Marshall
Fight Coach – James Binkley
Movement Coach – Clarence Ford

PLAYWRIGHT'S NOTES

Clout is an expressionistic comedy; the play takes place inside the head of a dying man on a morphine drip. The first production was staged in a black box setting with a stage element that lifted both horizontally and vertically. The lighting design emphasized the suspended quality of this limbo: we used only one blackout – all other transitions were on the fly. The sound score employed computer-manipulated riffs from a couple of well-known pop songs; the time in the music stretched and twisted like warm toffee to support the dream-like atmosphere of the piece. My music choices are obviously illustrative rather than prescriptive. We used the sound of dripping water in all the torture cell settings. Again, the sound source was manipulated to evoke the shifting colours of various psychological states. The overriding impression should be of story elements drifting through each other like twists of smoke. My stage directions and tech cues are the sign posts I needed to find my way through this netherworld and locate the initial production. I would urge you to ignore them if they get in the way and see the play the way you want to see it.

David Young, 15 February 2001

[MUSIC under. 'Walk Away, Renee' processional quiets the audience.]

[MUSIC out.]

ANNOUNCER: *[off]* ... And now, please welcome the Lord of Fleet Street, the darling of Wall Street, the champion of Main Street, the Chairman of the Board of Biggar International, Mr Lionel K. Biggar!

[MUSIC in: Nancy Sinatra, 'These Boots Were Made for Walking'.]

[Single SPOT: a lectern.]

[LIONEL BIGGAR enters the light dressed as Lord Nelson: wig, bicorne hat, frock coat, ruffled shirt, velvet breeches, silk hose, knee-high black patent leather boots. The MUSIC swells. Flashbulbs pop. Biggar vamps for the audience, demonstrating the power of his boots. Here is a man who takes enormous pleasure in the spotlight.]

BIGGAR: Ladies, gentlemen, fellow stakeholders of Biggar International, we have been accused of stuffiiness at our Annual General Meetings. This year I decided to do something about that. Since our colleagues in the soft-left media delight in portraying me as a myopic eighteenth-century baron, I thought, why not play the game?

[Biggar throws up his arms, gestures for applause. More flashbulbs.]

BIGGAR: According to the gurus of the 'Information Age', no one at this Annual General Meeting should be smiling.

It is our misfortune to own 437 newspapers and, as the experts are quick to remind us, in the Electronic Age print is a dead donkey. A sunset industry. Long term, our enterprise is doomed; we'll be swallowed whole like a chunk of carrion in some megadeal that trades on the magic words 'convergence' and 'synergy'. *[pause, smile]* I think not. You see, we thrive where others sicken and die. We have doubled in size twice in the last ten years. Some thirty million subscribers worldwide. Everywhere that sunshine falls upon this earth people are reading our newspapers. It is called 'clout' and we purchased it at knock-down prices.

We will not apologize for our successes. Life is about winning. Show me a good loser and I will show you a loser.

My friends, if we succeed it is because we take our responsibilities as publisher seriously. You are my shareholders. I am your servant. Together, we are the custodians of precious freedoms. We must speak to the perils of our day – which brings me nicely to the central thrust of my remarks this afternoon. Other owners of media outlets may choose to espalier their public pronouncements along the picket fence of the reigning liberal orthodoxy. That sort of relativistic equivocation is not my style. *[pause]* I prefer plain speech. What needs to be said is that our society teeters on the brink of a New Dark Age.

I will not stand by and watch as the lights of our great civilization are put out one by one. It will not happen. Not on my watch.

We have our enemies, people who wish to thwart us – some of them are here in the hall with us ... Mr Salutin ... Mr Saul ... Ms McQuaig ... *[whipping his back]* chh-chhh-chh.

[A man in the front row, TRENT, *wearing a toque and a greasy bathrobe, cranks around to look into the audience.]*

BIGGAR: Who are these so-called citizens who would thwart the will of you, my shareholders? They swarm under the linoleum in our publishing houses, television stations, museums, art galleries and universities. They are the pusillanimous pussyfooters who crowd the corridors of our bureaucracies. They are the unctuous cultural hucksters who manufacture and manipulate symbols for a living. They are the envious. They are the mediocre. Their empty slogans – *[mocking]* 'North-South', 'the politics of meaning', 'the Third Way' – are an ideological bathtub ring left over from the sixties. They unleash upon us the howling mob of compulsive do-gooders and guilt-mongering victims who would strip you of the profits of our enterprise! Let me enumerate them, the fallen angels who goose step on the head of the proverbial pin: *[accelerating cadence]* militant homosexuals seeking civil liberties for deviants, sagging feminists whining about the evils of patriarchy, abortionists playing God with the unborn, chinless eco-geeks wringing their hands about the ozone hole, welfare addicts showing us their bedsores, native people mewling about paleolithic utopias, jackbooted union thugs – the whole seething mob of 'victims' swarming up in tribal rage, shrieking with one shrill voice about compassion and caring and sharing and ME – ME – ME! *[pause]* SILENCE! ALL OF YOU! BE FOREWARNED!

[Pause.]

BIGGAR: You have snatched the hood from a falcon ... The central question: How do we defend our civilization against the me-Me-ME-ism that threatens to destroy it?

The simple answer: A qualifying exam for adulthood.

Why should all the hard-won freedoms of citizenship be a gift of birth? This is a crusty old proposition tested these several centuries and found wanting. It is time to stop the madness. The world is not fair. People are not as sweet and responsible as we thought they were. The democratic experiment needs a new set of rules.

A qualifying exam for adulthood!

You can't drive a car without a driver's licence, why should you have the right to vote, own property or bear arms, much less children, without proving, in a well-crafted written exam, that you are capable of assuming the duties and responsibilities of adulthood?

TRENT: *[interrupting]* HORSE SHIT!

[Trent stands up in the aisle.]

TRENT: Justify your pay packet, Biggar.

BIGGAR: Aha, aha, yes ... Mr Trent, former syndicated columnist, recently fired by the *Chronicle*. It's been thirty-two years, has it not? Photographic memory.

TRENT: Ewww, Lionel K. Biggar's brain. We are soooo afraid. We've had it with the pontification, okay? Justify your pay packet, Big Guy! We're all listening.

BIGGAR: You are an unemployed journalist, and you have come to disrupt these proceedings. Is that a bathrobe? How picturesque.

TRENT: Your company is awash in debt. Your stock is in the toilet. You paid yourself fifteen million bucks last year. You spent forty-five million on a new corporate jet. *[to audience]* He laid off nearly four hundred journalists last year!

BIGGAR: Three hundred and sixty-two.

TRENT: Hates democracy! Too much noise and confusion! Shut it down! *[brandishing manuscript]* I've written a book about you!

[Biggar gestures grandly, throwing a SPOT *on Trent.]*

BIGGAR: Evict this man from the premises!

TRENT: I – I – I ...

[Trent waves his open palms in a panic. LIGHT *shifts, Biggar freezes. We are in a different space-time. Trent is caught in his pool of light.]*

*[*AUDIO HALLUCINATION*: hospital beeps. Trent looks around, confused: his bathrobe, the manuscript, the surrounding darkness.]*

TRENT: Nurse? Nurse!

NURSE: *[off]* I'll be right there, Mr Trent.

[Trent thumbs his manuscript in a panic, looking for his place.]

TRENT: *[muttering search]* You stand accused – you stand accused – you stand accused … the run-in … here … I – I know nothing of your book, sir. I am merely trying to restore order at a public meeting …

[Trent waves his arm again. LIGHT *shifts to AGM levels. Biggar comes out of his freeze.]*

BIGGAR: I know nothing of your book, sir. I am merely trying to restore order (at a public meeting).

TRENT: *[interrupting]* No publisher in the country will touch it. 'Oh no, Mr Biggar might sue for libel. Even if you're totally innocent it would cost hundreds of thousands to defend you.' Can't say this, daren't say that – he shuts down public debate!

BIGGAR: Mr Trent –

TRENT: You stand accused!

[Trent gasps for air, drops to one knee.]

BIGGAR: Of what, my dear man, having more than you? I could not have less, for you have nothing at all except an overweening envy that masquerades as moral indignation –

TRENT: *[gasping]* No – no – no, that's not how it goes …

[Trent tries to balance his breathing.]

TRENT: Nurse …

BIGGAR: I achieved and you did not, therefore I must be thwarted. The world doesn't work that way any more, Mr Trent. You have lost touch.

[Trent stands, struggles for breath. He takes off his toque. Chemo has denuded him.]

TRENT: You, sir, are a danger to democracy.

BIGGAR: *[gentle]* Please take note, envy and moral superiority do not issue from the underclass, but from our so-called intellectual elites. These rabble-rousers have held centre court for the last fifty years masquerading as guardians of some self-serving 'common good'. One wearies of their intellectual hooliganism. *[secret smile]* Sooner or later, someone had to drown the kittens.

[SOUND: supportive applause.]

TRENT: NO!

[Trent waves his open palms in a fury. LIGHT shifts to vignette Biggar, who freezes. Trent mounts stairs to the stage. He examines Biggar like a statue in a museum.]

TRENT: You're a hard man to get at, Lionel K. Biggar. We rabble-rousers shoot our arrows over the castle wall and hope for the best. On a personal level, I can tell you there comes a time when that isn't enough. I'm storming your palace of lies. A writer's freedom, sir, to stir time and space with a fingertip. The world order you embrace – economic freedom without social responsibility – is not inevitable. Your ideology is not only wrong, it is dangerously wrong. All of this will be revealed … in the pages of my book …

[He prepares to release him.]

TRENT: Even here, under my total control, you are a wily and dangerous adversary. New setting! 'Nor can I give you back your job, Mr Trent …'

[He waves his open palms again, releasing Biggar from his pose. The light doesn't return to AGM levels.]

BIGGAR: *[mid-thought]* – nor can I give you back your job, Mr Trent, or promise I won't sue you if you … *[Biggar looks around, confused]* … if you libel me. Anything else? Good. Let's give this poor chap a warm round of –

[Biggar starts to applaud, turns to the surrounding darkness. He's spooked now.]

TRENT: *[pleased]* So …

BIGGAR: Wait a minute … who? Where? Security!

TRENT: We're in my brain, Biggar. Hating you keeps me alive.

BIGGAR: What a terrible curse upon your life, my dear fellow. That wristband – you escaped from a mental hospital. I want you to just be calm. You are clearly in some distress at the present moment. I know a thing or two about acupressure points.

[Biggar stalks him, holding out his thumb like a weapon.]

TRENT: The oncology unit. Small cell tumour, anterior lobe of the right lung. Cisplatinum chemo. Radiation. Morphine speedballs. Pack my sinuses with rat poison, I said, it's not about quality of life. Keep me on this plane of being until my manuscript is published; after that, bring down the vultures!

BIGGAR: We shall see what my security detail has to say about your presence here on this 'plane of being'.

TRENT: *[mocking]* 'My security detail'. Do you ever listen to yourself, Biggar? The grandiose assumptions! The boundless arrogance! Who do you think you are?

BIGGAR: I am one of the most powerful men on this planet.

[SOUND: a deep rumble from the bowels of the earth.]

[They are both startled. The floor starts to shake. LIGHTS flicker.]

TRENT: Holy shit. Holy shit!

BIGGAR: Earthquake!

[SOUND: Treated guitar riffs from 1968. The birthing cries of the earth. A dangerous radiance. Steel girders creak and groan. Dogs bark. Roosters crow. The lectern topples. Biggar grabs Trent for support. The big shock hits. Trent and Biggar are knocked to their knees.]

[SOUND: a crack of thunder; a lightning flash knocks out the LIGHTS momentarily. They come back on to reveal EVE, lithe and agile as an acrobat, as she lands in front of Biggar and Trent. She is wearing a camouflage jumpsuit, a mask over her face.]

EVE: ON THE FLOOR! HANDS BEHIND YOUR HEADS!

TRENT: Who – who, what – ?

EVE: SHUT UP! You are under MY control!

BIGGAR: Help! HELP!

[Eve hits Biggar's arm with an injection device. He clutches Trent and topples sideways.]

TRENT: I have nothing to do with –

EVE: SHUT UP!

[She injects Trent. He goes down atop Biggar. She puts her boot on them.]

EVE: NO GOD! NO MASTERS! NO LAWS!

[SNAP TO BLACK.]

[MUSIC: *electronic musical ramp to indicate shifting space and time. This music cue is built around a sampled/looped version of the descending bass riff from 'These Boots Are Made for Walking'.]*

[LIGHTS *shift.]*

[Biggar and Trent are sprawled on the floor, hooded and handcuffed back to back. They come around slowly, groggy with drug hangovers.]

[SOUND: *cooing baby.]*

TRENT: *[coming to consciousness]* Who? What? When? Where? How? *[pause]* Why?

[Trent struggles, arousing Biggar.]

TRENT: Help! HELP!

BIGGAR: Shut up!

TRENT: Where – where are we?

BIGGAR: Hush!

*[*SOUND*: a roll of distant thunder.]*

[A GIRL *sings the opening lines from 'These Boots Are Made for Walking'.]*

*[*SOUND*: the tinkle of wind chimes. The storm has passed.]*

TRENT: Holy shit, what is happening? We're spinning out of control here ... help, HELP!

[Trent's breathing shortens, he flops around. Biggar struggles to sit upright.]

BIGGAR: BE STILL! *[to himself]* This thirst ...

*[*SOUND WITH ECHO*: drip-drip-drip of water to create the audio illusion of a dank cave. The* CUE *plays intermittently through the rest of the act.]*

*[*SINGLE *on a white plastic pail. A luminous icon.]*

EVE: *[whisper, off]* Who ... tells ... the story?

[Drip. Drip. Drip.]

TRENT: Can't breathe … this hood … are you hooded?

BIGGAR: You can drop the bloody charade. I know your game.

TRENT: Pardon me?

BIGGAR: You were the decoy.

TRENT: Excuse me?

BIGGAR: I am not naïve, sir. You were part of the snatch team.

TRENT: Rest assured, this is entirely beyond my control, Biggar. We're in uncharted territory here.

[Trent fights to take off his hood.]

TRENT: No air …

[The hood comes off. Trent is no longer wearing his toque. He looks dreadful.]

BIGGAR: How much money did they offer you?

TRENT: I had nothing to do with this … I mean, granted, I set this scenario in motion, the Annual General Meeting, you in your cocked-up Lord Nelson rig with the Nancy Sinatra soundtrack … I – I was in control but then the story sort of twisted back on itself. *[pause]* My mind is a hall of mirrors.

BIGGAR: Your mind is a puddle of curdled dog vomit. I am soooo glad I fired you, Mr Trent. I did, you know, personally. It's one of the reasons I purchased that nickel-dime chain of newspapers. To get at hacks like you. The mocking class.

[Trent examines a wide belt around his middle that's attached to a canvas diaper-like appurtenance.]

TRENT: This diaper thing ... have they got you wearing a diaper? Seen them in the prisoner's dock. Electrified restraints. Look, for crissakes!

[He tries to take off Biggar's hood.]

BIGGAR: Take your dirty, filthy paws off me!

[They struggle. Trent pulls off Biggar's hood.]

TRENT: We could be in for some pain here, Lionel. *[pause]* You might like that.

[Biggar jerks Trent's arms, causing him pain. Drip. Drip. Drip.]

BIGGAR: You have no idea what you've gotten yourself into here. I have been trained in these matters. There will be no surprises. The fact that simple envy could lead you to participate in an act of such utter idiocy ...

TRENT: I don't envy you, Biggar. I know far too much.

BIGGAR: Pffht. You know nothing about me.

TRENT: I can't wait until you read my book – it's all there. Like so many of our pedigreed tycoons, the best decision you ever made was choosing your parents. The Consolidated Coal fortune lands in your lap at age twenty-four. Born on third base, spends his life thinking he hit a triple. You paid a terrible price for the privilege of your birthright, Lionel. Cheated out of a normal childhood, the pathetic spectacle of your mother bursting open like an overripe melon. In childhood you were loveless and alone, thus the grotesque deformations of character you manifest as an adult.

BIGGAR: Psycho-babbling nitwit.

TRENT: 'I am one of the most powerful men on this planet.' You make a fool of yourself every time you open your mouth in public. No one takes you seriously.

[Trent laughs.]

BIGGAR: We'll see who takes me seriously.

[Biggar snaps Trent into the crucifixion pose.]

TRENT: Aha, there it is, anger, anger, anger. I understand, Lionel. You have everything a man could want, all the ten thousand small advantages, a parallel private universe that is arranged entirely for your benefit – and yet you feel cheated. You were cheated, Lionel. Nothing can fill the hole in your soul. That's why you seek total control. *[feigning agony]* Release my arms. Please. I – I am a dying man.

[Biggar buys the ruse and releases him. Trent is pleased.]

[Drip. Drip. Drip.]

TRENT: You're not all bad, Lionel. Nobody is. It's just that your central belief –

BIGGAR: My central belief is that the people who own the world ought to govern it.

TRENT: All power in the hands of the mighty members of the Lucky Sperm Club and their political flunkies? Don't count on it, Big Guy.

BIGGAR: Who will stop me? Some pathetic little worm in a ratty bathrobe?

[Trent reaches down and scratches his crotch, taking Biggar's hand with him.]

TRENT: The multitudes beyond the castle wall. This world belongs to us. We don't need your permission to be on the premises. We want bread. We want roses. We shall have both.

[Biggar realizes he is helping to scratch Trent's crotch.]

BIGGAR: The stone-throwing mob ...

TRENT: Thanks. Fungal infection. I'm not supposed to scratch it. *[Biggar reacts with horror.]* You want to cut the cords that bind the family of man. I'm going to make an example of you, Lionel K. Biggar.

BIGGAR: Oh, now I'm really scared.

TRENT: I think you'll be impressed with the way I've deployed my materials. Our relationship, all the way back. *[the sweet secret]* There's a whole chapter devoted to your run for the student council presidency in 1968.

BIGGAR: Do you actually remember 1968? I think not. You were smoking copious amounts of marijuana on a couch in the seedy editorial office of a campus newspaper. You were reading the letters of Che Guevera aloud to your harem. *[the deep secret]* Renee.

TRENT: You dare to speak her name?

[Drip. Drip. Drip.]

TRENT: I think about her at the oddest moments. She sort of wafts through.

BIGGAR: Well, well, the glimmer of a guilty conscience.

TRENT: My conscience is clear.

BIGGAR: The incalculable suffering –

TRENT: Entirely your responsibility.

BIGGAR: You infected her with your libertine ideas.

TRENT: You poisoned her with your money. Remember that photograph you sent me, Biggar? That little twist of the knife? It's in the book, page 147. 'College love nest ends in tragedy.'

BIGGAR: Perverted bastard.

[They struggle for control.]

TRENT: You will NEVER silence me!

[Trent struggles against Biggar, gains ground inch by inch.]

TRENT: *[clenched teeth]* Focus ... focus ... focus.

BIGGAR: Blood sugar ...

[A Mexican standoff. Trent brims with fanatic energy. He pulls Biggar's arms back inch by inch. Biggar is stunned by Trent's strength.]

TRENT: Riddled with cancer rot, and he DOMINATES!

[Drip. Drip. Drip. AUDIO HALLUCINATION*: hospital.]*

TRENT: Nurse! Nurse?

[Trent scratches his crotch. Biggar pulls his hand away.]

TRENT: Oh, thanks, man. I really shouldn't do that. It's got to scab over.

[Drip. Drip. Drip.]

BIGGAR: I must have some food. Do you have any food?

TRENT: You want to eat at a time like this?

BIGGAR: Intolerable thirst ...

[He scopes out the pail with the dripping water. His thirst builds.]

*[*SOUND*: cooing baby.]*

TRENT: That baby again ...

[Biggar heads for the pail, dragging Trent behind.]

BIGGAR: A tactic. Disorient me. Break me down.

TRENT: With a baby?

BIGGAR: Genuine kidnappers and terrorists are ruthless bastards. The Baader-Meinhof gang liked to push baby carriages in front of limousines. The driver would squeal to a stop. They'd rake the vehicle with machine-gun fire.

TRENT: Fanatics trying to hijack the collective narrative. Exactly your game, Biggar.

BIGGAR: Excuse me? 'Collective narrative'?

[Biggar sucks water droplets out of the air.]

TRENT: You hate the word 'collective', don't you?

BIGGAR: I associate it with an infestation of lice.

TRENT: The collective narrative is the transcendent story that binds us together and provides a basis for moral conduct. Every society has one. You want to delete crucial sections of the story, rewrite the past so you can control the future and get rid of the lice once and for all. All six billion of us.

BIGGAR: Sounds like a plan.

TRENT: 'The democratic experiment needs a new set of rules.' A seismic shift in world reality, we are told, and it is a good thing. Let economics be the first and only law. Bow down, ye faithful, before the almighty god of globalization! Compete or die! Cut the fat! Dismantle all programs that serve the common good – too expensive, you fool! We're up against Taiwan! The kids over there sleep under their workbenches! And, oh yeah, I'll be seein' y'all real soon. I'm hoppin' the Gulfstream Five to Singapore for an important lunch with the *[sings]* Duke – Duke – Duke – Duke of Earl. *[pause]* What the fuck are you doing?

BIGGAR: Do you ever shut up?

TRENT: Infrequently.

[Drip. Drip. Drip.]

BIGGAR: I must eat something.

TRENT: *[innocent]* I have a bit of food.

BIGGAR: You do?

TRENT: A Tootsie Roll.

BIGGAR: You have a Tootsie Roll?

TRENT: Mm-hm. The morphine drip gives me the sugar munchies. *[producing it]* Bit of tobacco stuck to it, otherwise ...

BIGGAR: Give it to me.

TRENT: Oh, really ...

BIGGAR: Right away. Now. NOW!

TRENT: Forget it.

[Biggar starts to dig at Trent's fist. A struggle.]

TRENT: I'm not sharing my Tootsie Roll with you, man!

BIGGAR: Give it to me!

TRENT: Fuck you!

[Biggar bites down on Trent's hand, grabs the Tootsie Roll that falls loose and sucks at it feverishly.]

TRENT: Greedy bastard!

BIGGAR: *[panting, sucking]* I have a lazy pancreas.

[Trent digs at his crotch, knowing Biggar is too busy to stop him.]

TRENT: Really? Borderline diabetes? How could I not know that?

BIGGAR: My, my, a tiny blank in your panoramic understanding of my life.

[Drip. Drip. Drip.]

TRENT: Real question: Do you think Renee ever loved you?

[Trent's scratching increases to fever pitch. Biggar realizes his hand is in Trent's crotch.]

BIGGAR: What?

[He whips it clear.]

BIGGAR: You are a perverted sex fiend.

TRENT: I loved her. I mean, I really loved her. I don't think she ever believed that.

BIGGAR: Didn't you see the way she was smiling in that photograph? Her feelings for me verged on obsession, which in the fullness of time came to be something of a problem.

TRENT: In your dreams.

[Drip. Drip. Drip.]

TRENT: Where was that photograph taken?

BIGGAR: A cozy little cottage in Ingonish. Wind chimes on the front porch. Waterbed in the living room. Oh, the rapture of it ...

[Drip. Drip. Drip.]

TRENT: Boy or girl?

BIGGAR: Imagine not knowing that. Are you capable of shame?

TRENT: It was your show.

BIGGAR: You had duties and responsibilities.

TRENT: We're getting off topic. I – I've already put paid to the sixties. That chapter is written and polished to a high sheen.

BIGGAR: Come on then, let's hear it, the polished version.

TRENT: You'll read it when I publish my book. Chapter Five.

BIGGAR: You admit there may be legal impediments to the publication of said manuscript. It's just the two of us here – tell me what you wrote. 1968. Start at the beginning.

[Drip. Drip. Drip. Trent is confused.]

TRENT: I – I've had some memory lapses. The morphine drip.

BIGGAR: You really don't remember, do you? The Hunt Club. You wore a white waiter's jacket and brought us our drinks. That's how it began.

TRENT: Wrong.

BIGGAR: Photographic memory, Mr Trent. It's all in here. Every doorway. Every whiskey and soda. Every grand prospect across a spreading lawn. You in your white waiter's jacket, it's too short in the sleeve. You looked ridiculous. All your grandiose Marxist posturing and there you are, a hired monkey serving champagne to the rich.

TRENT: You in your fucking Bentley, some weird bit of aristocratic upchuck.

BIGGAR: You think you can just say anything here, don't you?

TRENT: That's the beauty of this little tableau vivant. There is nothing outside the envelope of my thinking.

BIGGAR: What makes you think you're not INSIDE the envelope of MY thinking?

TRENT: What a disgusting thought.

[Drip. Drip. Drip. Biggar sucks his candy noisily.]

BIGGAR: *[whisper]* Here's the straight story. I have a multinational security detail: agents recruited from Mossad and the SAS. The crème de la crème of international antiterrorist operatives.

TRENT: *[pleased]* Sounds like a detail I'd invent.

BIGGAR: These are top people, Mr Trent. They know all the variables. They have walked me through all the scenarios. The last time we went on exercise I was tortured for a week in the basement of an English country house.

TRENT: Most excellent.

BIGGAR: I'm telling you the truth. What we are experiencing here is a real-time simulation. That masked woman is an employee of mine and I know what is about to unfold here, which makes it far worse. Seeing the future. Godlike. Terrifying. That's what these training exercises are all about, you see. Helping me push my limits well beyond those of any mortal man. Torture is all about boundaries. Repetition and anticipation. Pain, wait. Pain, wait. The object of the exercise is to open the gates of time and enter the eternal present. An ancient trance state, Mr Trent, the anteroom of the great beyond.

TRENT: Really?

BIGGAR: Mayan kings ate magic mushrooms and pierced their foreskins with the barbed spear of the stingray to get where we are going.

TRENT: *[spooked]* You've lost your mind.

BIGGAR: On the contrary, I am here to watch you lose yours, Mr Trent. You will experience indescribable pain, pain so sharp it will cut the cord that binds mind to body. You will stand outside yourself. That's the worst of it, standing apart at the very end while those dreadful final screams pour out of your body ...

[Biggar makes a terrible throttled noise in his throat.]

BIGGAR: *[whisper]* At Culloden the Scottish warriors bit out the throats of the enemy. I vividly remember reading that as a young lad. I could see it in my mind's eye. I wanted to try it. Imagine the frenzy.

TRENT: Stop!

BIGGAR: I know what I want and I can afford to pay for it. At the end of this scenario our hostess is going to make me bite out your tongue. This will happen before you are dead, Mr Trent. That is how they play the game in the real world, you see. They take away speech. A final insult to your departing soul. And my job is to play my role without caving in. That's what this is all about, you see. They want me to experience every hideous moment as you are tortured to death ... it's a kind of final exam for those who want to play the game at the highest level, Mr Trent. Are you ready to play the game?

[Trent cowers. Biggar laughs, the game is over.]

BIGGAR: Beware your thoughts, Mr Trent. I may have put them in your head. *[whisper]* I stir time and space with my fingertip.

TRENT: *[weakening]* Dream on.

BIGGAR: We shall see.

[Drip. Drip. Drip.]

*[*SOUND*: distorted water drops become the echo of approaching footsteps.]*

[Biggar falls over on his side, dragging Trent down with him.]

BIGGAR: *[whisper]* We're asleep.

[Eve enters. She's dressed entirely in black, wearing a mask with holes for the eyes and mouth. She carries a large black duffel bag. She takes in the scene.]

[Drip. Drip. Drip.]

[Biggar snores. Trent scratches his crotch.]

EVE: Who took off the hoods?

[They both snore theatrically. Biggar pulls his hand away from Trent's crotch. She drops the bag. It clanks.]

EVE: Who moved the pail?

[No response. She adjusts settings on something that looks like a TV *remote control, then pushes buttons to activate their restraint belts. They react violently to the jolts of electricity. She stops. They pant.]*

EVE: First rule: When she asks a question, she gets an answer. Electrified nappies. Who took off the hoods?

BIGGAR: He did.

EVE: Who moved the pail?

TRENT: He did.

EVE: Mutual finger pointing. Perfect. I've had you boys under high magnification. My two little bugs.

[She strolls around them.]

EVE: Who am I? Where are we? What's going to happen?

[She menaces them with her stun unit.]

EVE: Agenda, agenda, who's got the agenda? Who's got a believable scenario? Anybody know where we are or why we're here? I mean, could somebody float a theory for me? *[to Biggar]* Why are we here? That's a question.

BIGGAR: I presume you're both part of a kidnapping team that seeks some sort of ransom.

TRENT: He thinks I'm in league with you.

[Eve laughs at that idea.]

BIGGAR: I am well schooled in the modus operandi of snatch teams.

EVE: So I hear, the English country house. My, my. Or did he make that up? *[adjusts her unit]* He was on three. Here's a four. Dance, partner.

[She gives Trent a quick series of jolts.]

TRENT: See, smarty pants?

EVE: Good recovery time.

[She gives Trent another quick jolt.]

EVE: *[in Biggar's face]* New territory, Lionel. Forget ransom. Think reckoning, as in final. Think – *[to Trent]* what did he call it? – a qualifying exam for adulthood? That sounds about right. Does anybody here qualify as an adult?

TRENT: *[panic]* It's just as you said, she's your employee. This is an elaborate real-time simulation, like that dungeon weekend at the English country house.

EVE: Fair enough. Let's take that scenario for a ride. I'm your employee. You're to be tested at the highest level. I torture you, he witnesses, we open the gates of time and enter the ancient trance. What do you say, Lionel? *[pause]* That was a question.

BIGGAR: You must contact my people and make your demands. I assure you they will co-operate fully with –

EVE: 'My people'?

TRENT: Gotta love him.

EVE: Was I talking to you?

[She gives Trent a JOLT. *And another. And another. And another.]*

EVE: My thumb's gonna get sore.

[Trent flops around like a rag doll, convulsing in spasms of pain, that horrible strangling sound pouring out of his throat.]

BIGGAR: Stop this at once!

[She stops.]

EVE: Does that sound make you uncomfortable, Lionel? Surely not. That's what you hear when you stand on the prow of time. Those dots down there are human beings.

BIGGAR: I'm afraid I don't entirely grasp your objectives here.

EVE: We're deep in a mystery, Lionel. Somebody's been rewriting my history. I'm going to get to the bottom of it. I'll be reaching into your hearts, your minds. Rest assured, we'll have some new experiences.

BIGGAR: May I remind you that your ransom negotiations will depend entirely upon my being in good health. My people will not pay for damaged goods.

EVE: You won't have a mark on you. *[taps forehead]* The real boundaries are up here, right?

[Eve laughs, moves off.]

EVE: See this black bag? When I move toward it you, start to sweat, okay? That is my advice to you.

TRENT: Please …

[Eve rummages in the bag.]

EVE: What's your problem? Personal martyrdom, a perfect ending for the story you've been telling yourself all these years. Shall we begin? Are we ready to play at the highest level?

[She turns to them, revealing a large pair of forceps and a lash.]

EVE: These do a nice job.

[She puts the lash aside and menaces them with the forceps.]

EVE: *[whisper]* Pain, wait. Pain, wait. Only one way to enter this world. So many ways to leave. A difficult passage …

BIGGAR: You must call my people.

EVE: *[to Trent]* We've got our work cut out for us here. It will take time and patience but, believe me, a man of this calibre is trainable.

TRENT: I – I believe we are all capable of change.

EVE: A simple little shift of emphasis. *[makes fist]* This – *[open palm]* to this. I like to start here *[indicates webbing between thumb and first finger]*. A very rich complex of nerve endings.

[Eve applies her forceps to Trent's hand. He screams in agony. She watches Biggar. No reaction. She presses harder. Trent slumps, quivering. She withdraws.]

[Drip. Drip. Drip. She taps the top of Biggar's head in time with the drips.]

EVE: Wait. Wait. Wait. *[whisper]* 'I take away all your choices. You've never felt so free.' Do you remember saying those words?

[Biggar is unnerved.]

EVE: One of your famous sayings. The most powerful man on the planet.

TRENT: You should read my book. There's a fantasy sequence, Lionel K. Biggar hosting a party at Davos in a black latex catsuit. Large and in charge.

EVE: *[laughs]* You are a funny boy.

TRENT: Thank you.

BIGGAR: Apply your instrument to his earlobe.

EVE: Yes, sir.

[She does so. Trent screams and whimpers. She increases the pressure. Trent starts to speak in tongues. Terrifying. Eve watches Biggar's face.]

BIGGAR: Enough!

[Drip. Drip. Drip.]

BIGGAR: What are your demands?

EVE: Let's go big picture, Lionel. I mean, you've got a zillion dollars and all the newspapers and the model trains and the private jet and the 180-foot yacht and the homes all over the world and the interlocking directorships with your rich and powerful friends. For a person of my background there's a lot not to like ... what really concerns me is that you and Mother Nature seem to be on a bit of a collision course.

BIGGAR: I have no idea what you're talking about.

[She applies the pliers to the tip of his nose.]

EVE: There are people in this world who have worn out their welcome, my friend, and you are one of them. We're not going to let you melt the ice caps. That's the bottom line.

TRENT: He thinks global warming is an intellectual fad. There's a whole chapter in my book about it. He's an aberration of nature. A creature who eats the world and shits money.

EVE: Funny boy.

TRENT: I'm a satirist. I live for the sound of your laughter. Who erected Nelson's Column? *[pause]* Lady Hamilton.

[She laughs.]

EVE: I feel a familiarity with you. That might mean something. A thread in the larger mystery ...

TRENT: That would be wonderful.

[She musses Biggar's hair. He fumes in silence.]

EVE: Quite the unit, isn't he?

TRENT: I love the photographic memory bit. He can quote for hours from Samuel Johnson and the *Meditations* of Marcus Aurelius. Lay it on her, Big Guy.

BIGGAR: *[quoting]* 'Adapt yourself to the environment in which your lot has been cast, and show true love to the fellow mortals with whom destiny has surrounded you.'

EVE: Ew, Lionel, I'm all wet.

TRENT: I'm having a good time here.

[Biggar jerks Trent's arms around.]

EVE: Naughty.

[She moves to rearrange their handcuffs.]

EVE: I better separate you two. Protective custody.

[They ad lib insults and leg-wrestle while she adjusts their shackles. Eve stands away. Trent is surprised to discover he is free. Biggar is handcuffed to a floor shackle. Trent stands, a funny reveal on his diaper belt. He goes at his crotch with a vengeance. Baboon time.]

BIGGAR: Aha, all is revealed at last, the inside story.

EVE: The inside story? Hardly. We're peeling a big onion here. *[to Trent]* Do you mind?

BIGGAR: Your allegiances are crystal clear.

EVE: I'm getting tired of this attitude. This entitlement. *[to Trent]* I want to play on your side of the table for a while. *[puts pliers between Biggar's legs]* Fresh oysters, anyone?

[Biggar is impassive.]

TRENT: No, please ...

EVE: You said hating him keeps you alive. Don't you want to hear those weird sounds pour out of his throat?

TRENT: I – I want him to change and become more fully human.

EVE: He's never going to change.

TRENT: I don't want to believe that. Change. Becoming. That's what makes the world go round.

BIGGAR: You suckhole.

EVE: Get over here and open his nappie. Last week a chunk of Antarctica the size of Belgium broke off and floated away into the South Atlantic. Do you, by any chance, have an editorial position?

[She buries the open pliers in Biggar's crotch. He doesn't blink.]

BIGGAR: Greenhouse gases, the last Trojan horse for the social engineers who want to dismantle the industrialized world and replace it with a state-controlled apparatus to redistribute wealth.

TRENT: *[mutter]* Stands by and applauds while the ice cap melts.

BIGGAR: I will not support the Jezebels of junk science.

EVE: We're talking about the fate of the earth.

BIGGAR: There is a natural ebb and flow in nature.

EVE: What?

BIGGAR: The earth warms and cools. The ice caps advance and retreat.

EVE: WHAT?

BIGGAR: There is no reliable evidence that so-called greenhouse gases –

EVE: BE SILENT!

[Eve swings her leg over Biggar's shoulder, catches his neck in a scissor hold and flexes her thighs.]

EVE: The global economy is a doomsday machine run by men.

[Biggar does a disjointed dance for a moment and goes limp. She keeps up the pressure. Trent is thunderstruck.]

EVE: One Mississippi, two Mississippi, three Mississippi, four Mississippi –

TRENT: What – what are you doing?

EVE: I'm cutting off the blood supply to his massive brain. It's a timing thing. *[loosens her grip and steps away]* He'll be out for five minutes.

[She moves around Trent.]

TRENT: *[nervous laugh]* You really had me going there when you were playing along with him, I mean, that bit about this being a real-time simulation organized by his security detail.

EVE: Games inside games.

[Drip. Drip. Drip.]

TRENT: I – I'm not sure about very much at the present moment ... my grasp ... I mean, is any of this ... real?

[She gives him a long look.]

EVE: How'd you get so lost?

TRENT: I've been under some stress. A change in my drinking pattern after I got fired. The manuscript became something of an obsession. No publisher would touch it. I – I lost the courage of my convictions. Bingo, tumour time! Anger, that's the common chord. Anger, anger, anger. Everything comes from anger.

EVE: Now you've lost me.

TRENT: I lie in my bed. The ceiling tiles pulse in and out. There is a rather alarming gap. A rupture in the fabric of space-time. I pass in and out of mental states. The wash of various emotions. The enduring impression is that all of this might be a product of my thinking, my need to think, the creaking Cartesian duality. Is the world composed of ideas ... or is it composed of things? *[touches his skull]* If it's all pure thought, then ...

EVE: Are you, by any chance, an intellectual?

TRENT: Intellectual, socialist, romantic and honorary lesbian.

[Eve laughs. He smiles.]

EVE: Such charm, such savoir faire. And this is how it looks ...

[She vamps him.]

TRENT: Burn out before you rust out.

EVE: I guess you broke a few hearts in your time.

TRENT: Broken hearts are an unfortunate by-product of left-wing politics. It's all about change and becoming. *[pause]* People get left behind.

EVE: What's one human heart when you're building the New Jerusalem?

[SHIMMER OF GHOSTLY MUSIC*: the chorus of 'Walk Away, Renee'.]*

[Trent reacts to the memory. She circles him.]

EVE: So. Go on, then. It's just the two of us. Seduce me with your thinking. Tell me what you believe.

TRENT: The object of the exercise is human progress. I've spent my life assembling ideas that will bring people together and make them more aware of their shared journey.

EVE: How would you feel if I fell in love with him instead?

TRENT: Huge error. Our friend here has spent his life building higher and higher walls behind which he hoards his wealth and power. *[himself]* Ideas. *[Biggar]* Things. The realist. *[himself]* The idealist. The future. The past. We are born enemies.

EVE: You like that, don't you? The 'us against them' stuff. I mean, that really is the central theme, isn't it?

TRENT: I don't even own a couch. Lionel K. Biggar purchased an entire Greek temple. He saw the bloody thing from his yacht. The locals hacked it out of the hillside with chainsaws. It's in his backyard! I didn't make this up ...

[Drip. Drip. Drip.]

TRENT: Or – or maybe I did ...

EVE: Huh?

TRENT: I'm hurtling toward the end of time. In the run-up to the final desperate hour one longs for ... for some kind of transformation ...

EVE: Transformation. What a concept.

TRENT: *[secret]* There's a great temptation to massage the data.

EVE: Huh?

TRENT: I made my choices. Did any of it matter? What is my legacy? I lie here in my bed, the morphine drip, the ceiling tiles pulsing in and out –

[She pinches him hard with the pliers. He drops to his knees with pain.]

EVE: Snap out of it, wanker! You're HERE. *[pause]* When were you born?

TRENT: 1946.

EVE: Same year as my dad. Baby-boom scum.

TRENT: Absolutely and totally couldn't agree with you more. Believe me, no one is more disappointed than me by my generation's utter abdication of –

EVE: *[interrupting]* You can be irritating. Did anyone ever tell you that?

TRENT: I can be a total weenie.

[Drip. Drip. Drip.]

EVE: Why are you looking at me like that?

TRENT: I want to understand. *[pause]* I am here for you.

[She gives him a long look.]

EVE: You'd like to go to bed with me, wouldn't you?

TRENT: I'd like to get to know you. We could see where that went.

EVE: You're old enough to be my father.

TRENT: Age is a relative thing.

[Drip. Drip. Drip.]

EVE: So? Shall we have sex?

TRENT: Here? Now?

EVE: Why not?

[Drip. Drip. Drip.]

TRENT: I – I'd need to tidy up a little.

[She moves around him. Drip. Drip. Drip.]

TRENT: You frighten me.

EVE: Good.

[Drip. Drip. Drip.]

TRENT: You've been involved in other kidnappings? *[no response]* You've been paid ransoms?

EVE: Gee, I guess we have.

TRENT: If I might ask, what do you do with the money?

EVE: We fund squads. Worldwide.

TRENT: Squads?

EVE: Eco-terrorists.

TRENT: Aha. I love what you kids are doing today.

EVE: Here we go, us against them.

[Biggar groans toward consciousness.]

EVE: I can keep a guy semi-conscious for hours. You want me to knock him out again?

TRENT: Let him come around.

EVE: I think I'd better set you a task, a test of character. You said you think he can change. All right. Bring him around to your way of thinking ... or what? Or watch him die, inch by inch. Ever seen a full-on diabetic seizure? It's the rabies movie. Very visceral. Very direct. Quite often they'll swallow their tongues. Look at you – burn out before you rust out – what a cutie.

[She pats Trent's head.]

EVE: Don't tell him we talked.

[She gives Biggar a jolt. Trent sneaks in some serious crotch scratching.]

EVE: Rise and shine, concubine.

[Biggar rises on one elbow. Groggy. Pulls against the floor shackle.]

EVE: *[to Trent]* Keep him out of trouble. Don't touch anything. *[pointedly]* Do not, repeat, do not drink the water.

[She exits.]

TRENT: Nurse? Nurse!

NURSE: *[pre-recorded voice]* Calm down, Mr Trent. You're having a restless night.

TRENT: I see your face ... everywhere.

NURSE: I'll be back soon.

[A pause. Biggar pulls against the floor shackle in a rage.]

BIGGAR: She has done something to my neck.

TRENT: She has enormously powerful thighs. We had a good talk. I think I made some headway.

BIGGAR: What were you talking about?

TRENT: Oh, this, that and the other. She is a deeply troubled young lady. The way I understand it, if you don't come around to MY way of thinking – I'm talking fundamental change here – she'll torture you to death. Very slowly.

BIGGAR: Oh. Really.

TRENT: The ice-cap issue. It's huge for her. Her people fund eco-terrorist units worldwide.

BIGGAR: She told you this?

TRENT: I was building a bridge of trust.

BIGGAR: You've set a new world record for the Stockholm Syndrome. Normally it takes months.

TRENT: I was only trying to determine how strongly bound she was to her group.

BIGGAR: There is no group, you dimwit! These people are rank amateurs.

TRENT: I don't think so.

BIGGAR: She's trailer park trash. A tool in the hands of 'some guy', and you, Mr Decoy, the disgruntled former employee. It doesn't take a genius to figure out this half-baked scenario.

TRENT: *[fed up]* Paranoid sociopath.

BIGGAR: Heinous brigand. If you think you'll get away with this ...

TRENT: Blame, blame, blame, blame, blame.

[Biggar takes a swipe at him. Trent dances out of reach.]

[Drip. Drip. Drip.]

[Biggar watches the drip. The bucket is just out of reach.]

BIGGAR: Get me the bucket.

TRENT: You heard her. Don't move anything. Don't drink the water.

BIGGAR: I am a borderline diabetic. I must have liquids or I go into a coma.

TRENT: She's monitoring the room.

[Biggar stretches. The bucket is an inch too far. Trent watches him with clinical interest.]

BIGGAR: *[to himself, with distress]* Starting to strobe ...

TRENT: Own who you are, man, or she will make you pay a terrible price.

BIGGAR: You'd stand there and watch me die in a diabetic seizure.

[Biggar is losing consciousness.]

TRENT: It's all so false. You preen and pose inside the soap bubble of your fame. Davos. Bilderberg. Lunch at the club in Kensington with Lady Thatcher. A snifter of brandy with Henry in your suite at the Pierre.

BIGGAR: *[fading fast]* There are only a handful of people who matter in this world.

TRENT: Tight corner, Big Guy. Come up with some fresh ideas about your place in the grand scheme of things. It's your only hope.

[Biggar appears to be out cold. Trent goes to him, concerned. Biggar lunges and grabs Trent by the ankle. Trent struggles to escape. Biggar works his way up Trent's leg.]

BIGGAR: Here comes Mr Crocodile. He's got Mr Bush Pig by the trotter. Drag him down to the green river, wedge him under a log, let the water soften him up.

[Wraps the chain around his neck.]

TRENT: *[strangled]* Help! Help!

BIGGAR: Is she an employee of mine, you imbecile?!

[Trent makes that terrible gurgling sound.]

BIGGAR: Or is all of this still happening in your drug-addled brain? Are you putting these words in my mouth? Hm?

TRENT: *[strangled]* I cannot … control … this … !

[Biggar tightens his grip.]

BIGGAR: One Mississippi. Two Mississippi. Three Mississippi.

TRENT: *[strangled]* Nurse! Nurse!

[Trent sags in Biggar's arms.]

*[*RENEE *enters stage left, dressed in an oversized man's white shirt and black jeans. She is an innocent eighteen-year-old college girl. Biggar stops choking Trent.]*

TRENT: Renee ...

[Biggar drops his shackles, taking charge of the moment.]

BIGGAR: You must be Renee. How lovely to see you. Look at you. Look at you.

RENEE: I didn't have the right outfit. I borrowed –

TRENT: That's my white shirt.

BIGGAR: Nonsense. You look – you look ... very ... very ... *you.* *[to Trent]* Waiter, I'm thirsty. Bring me champagne.

TRENT: Right away, sir.

[Trent steps out of the light. Renee is off balance in these surroundings.]

RENEE: What do they hunt?

BIGGAR: Pardon me?

RENEE: It's called the Hunt Club.

BIGGAR: Those who attend these premises do not hunt, my dear. They are bourgeois pretenders to the equestrian class in search of burled walnut marquetry, creaking leather club chairs and a glass of passable claret. We all play along.

RENEE: It's, um, it's nice. Are you a member?

BIGGAR: My grandfather founded the place. That's his portrait over the fireplace.

RENEE: What did he do?

BIGGAR: Mining engineer by profession, financier by temperament – at the end of the nineteenth century they called him the King of Carbon. First one to see the potential in the East Coast collieries. He blasted tunnels to follow the coal seams out under the Atlantic. He was pushing the engineering principles of the day and there were of course some catastrophic cave-ins. What?

RENEE: I'm not used to calling total strangers out of the blue.

BIGGAR: Never having received such a call, I welcomed it. It's nice to be noticed.

RENEE: You cut quite a figure, dashing across campus wearing that cape.

BIGGAR: Queen's Horse Guards. My Uncle Cecil was –

RENEE: *[interrupting]* You look like a kid playing Batman.

BIGGAR: Well, well.

RENEE: Nothing wrong with Batman. It suits you.

BIGGAR: *[nervous laugh]* I – I suppose I would hope to project a more nuanced public persona.

RENEE: I see people for who they are. You're the Caped Crusader.

[Biggar and Renee look in each other's eyes. Trent hovers, fascinated and appalled.]

RENEE: Never met a man I couldn't out-stare.

TRENT: Your champagne, sir.

RENEE: Trent, what are you doing here? I thought you only worked weekends.

TRENT: I'm a little short this month.

BIGGAR: You two know one another?

TRENT: *[frost]* Slightly.

RENEE: Trent edits the *Clarion*. I – I've done some sports writing.

BIGGAR: I see.

BIGGAR: *[toasting]* To nation builders.

RENEE: To blind dates.

TRENT: *[aside to Renee]* Nice shirt.

BIGGAR: You edit the campus newspaper? You are 'the editor'?

TRENT: It's an editorial collective, sir.

BIGGAR: Whatever that means in your corner of bohemia.

TRENT: It means we practise the principles of democracy, sir.

BIGGAR: Direct question: Are you personally in support of the anti-war propaganda that regularly seeps from the editorial pages of your so-called newspaper?

TRENT: I'm against the Vietnam War, sir, like most thinking people.

BIGGAR: You might find a few 'thinking people' in this jurisdiction who disagree with your newspaper's views.

TRENT: The war is evil, sir. We're going to stop it.

BIGGAR: So all of Asia can fall into the hands of the communist horde?

TRENT: You actually believe that horse shit, sir?

RENEE: *[to Trent]* Do we have to do this here, now?

TRENT: The Vietnam War is a vast money machine for a tiny corporate elite. Human blood greasing the wheels of industry!

RENEE: Trent has strong beliefs.

BIGGAR: I think the word is 'pungent'. *[Biggar and Renee laugh]* I'll tell you what I think. I think we should take the full fury of modern warfare to downtown Hanoi. We have weapons of mass destruction. We should use them. Boom boom boom. All better.

TRENT: *[to Renee]* You want to meet Satan? *[to Biggar]* America will lose the war. History will pass judgement on people like you.

BIGGAR: The victors will tell the story.

TRENT: You pig.

BIGGAR: I think I shall report you to the management. They may not fully understand who they've brought on staff here. Part-time.

RENEE: No, don't …

[SOUND up: sample from the Flamingos' 'I Only Have Eyes For You'.]

RENEE: *[to Biggar]* Let's dance.

[Biggar and Renee dance.]

TRENT: Aren't you going to introduce us?

RENEE: Lionel K. Biggar.

TRENT: Aha, the dude who tools around in the vintage Bentley. You're running for President of the Student Union.

BIGGAR: Indeed. And I assure you I shall win handily.

TRENT: We'll see about that.

[FRONT LIGHT on Trent, lying near the stage apron, apparently asleep. Renee kneels down beside him, hoping to creep into bed without waking him.]

TRENT: What time?

RENEE: After three.

TRENT: Where have you been?

RENEE: We stayed for the dance.

TRENT: Until three in the morning?

RENEE: I went back to his place.

TRENT: Lord Jesus.

RENEE: You wanted information about his campaign strategy. You told me to string him along.

TRENT: My tongue-in-cheek instructions were, 'Drop your pants for the cause, if that's what it takes'. You said, 'I'm not that kind of girl'. We had a laugh about it. You were humping the guy's leg!

RENEE: You taught me to dance.

[Trent turns away.]

RENEE: Why did you have to go shooting your mouth off? You were a step away from getting fired.

TRENT: I quit at the end of my shift.

RENEE: I thought you were broke.

[Pause.]

TRENT: So. What did you find out?

RENEE: He told me all about his life.

TRENT: Oh, really.

RENEE: It's a sad story, actually.

TRENT: How much did you have to drink?

RENEE: We shared a bottle of champagne.

TRENT: Softening you up.

RENEE: He was a perfect gentleman.

TRENT: 'I've never met a man I couldn't out-stare.'

RENEE: I don't believe it. You're jealous.

TRENT: Of that schmuck? Give me a break.

RENEE: You actually care.

TRENT: This isn't about you and me, okay? This is about the problem of evil. You were humping the guy's leg.

[Pause.]

RENEE: Please remember, this whole thing was your idea.

TRENT: What are his plans for the election?

RENEE: We didn't end up talking about that. We talked about his childhood.

TRENT: Fuck, fuck, FUCK! Spend six hours with the guy and he turns you around.

RENEE: His father died before he knew him. He was raised by an alcoholic mother.

TRENT: His mother was a screaming fascist bitch from hell – she put police dogs on striking coal miners! Three union organizers were killed in cold blood. These things happened!

RENEE: Trent –

TRENT: Lemme guess, while he was telling you all this he looked deep into your eyes and undid your bra strap with one hand –

RENEE: Go to hell.

TRENT: No, you go to hell.

[Trent turns away. He's insanely jealous.]

TRENT: I can't trust you.

RENEE: You can't trust anybody, Trent. Nobody measures up.

TRENT: You're a small-town girl. You came looking for a job on the paper because you wanted to go through some changes politically. I don't think you've got the chops for it. I think you're a girlie-girl.

RENEE: You and your labels.

TRENT: You were laughing at his jokes.

RENEE: Everything's got to fit into your little 'us against them' thing. It wears thin.

TRENT: I don't have to stay.

RENEE: No kidding.

[Pause.]

RENEE: I know who you really are. You say that's what you love about me.

TRENT: I don't want to be known by you.

[Renee bends to put her tongue in his ear.]

RENEE: Quit acting like a two-year-old. Nothing happened. We drank a bottle of wine. I talked to the guy. He's a human being.

[Trent rolls onto his back in the fetal position and sucks his thumb.]

TRENT: I'm Lionel K. Biggar and I've had it rough!

[She swats him. He grabs her.]

TRENT: Tell me you didn't kiss him.

RENEE: You want me to lie?

TRENT: You actually kissed Lionel K. Biggar.

RENEE: He kissed me, sort of.

TRENT: What do you mean, 'sort of'? A kiss is a kiss.

RENEE: He wasn't very good at it.

TRENT: Meaning?

RENEE: I can't believe you're being like this.

TRENT: Cheek or mouth?

RENEE: Mouth.

TRENT: Tongue?

RENEE: A little bit.

TRENT: Tell me *exactly* what happened.

RENEE: Lionel's got some sexual hang-ups.

TRENT: How do you know that?

RENEE: We talked about it.

TRENT: Were you standing, sitting or lying down?

RENEE: We were standing by the front door when it started. We ended up on the divan ...

TRENT: On the divan? This is a fucking nightmare! I want it moment by moment, okay? Leave nothing to my imagination.

[Renee stands up into the moment she has just described. Biggar is there.]

RENEE: Well, I – I guess I should be going.

[She gives Biggar a kiss on the cheek.]

TRENT: Wait a minute. You didn't say you kissed him.

RENEE: That was a peck on the cheek. Here comes the kiss.

[Biggar moves in with an awkward kiss on the mouth. Trent reacts with pain.]

BIGGAR: I – I don't know if I've ever felt like this.

RENEE: Like what?

BIGGAR: So ... 'go with the flow'.

TRENT: Lord help me.

RENEE: Well ... I certainly enjoyed myself.

TRENT: Why didn't you just leave?

RENEE: I liked the way he talked.

BIGGAR: It's difficult to explain my feelings, Renee. I have grown accustomed to a certain level of emotional renunciation.

RENEE: How do you mean?

TRENT: You're playing into the guy's hands.

BIGGAR: Certain aspects of human experience are foreign to me, Renee – out of bounds, if you will. I suppose I'm a solitary soul. I've never really known how to behave in the everyday world.

RENEE: You certainly seem to know what you want.

BIGGAR: There are some aspects of this life I understand all too well, Renee. The reach of ambition. The dimension of destiny. The chapters of my life are already written, you see. I merely turn the pages, trying to keep up with the story.

TRENT: Don't listen.

RENEE: My, my.

BIGGAR: I know, I know, it sounds ponderous, perhaps even pompous, but I read history, you see, I mean, I started as a young lad with the life of Lord Nelson and he became a kind of obsession for me until I knew so much about him that I could ascend the heights of his fame and see what he saw, other heroes on other mountaintops further back in time: Peter the Great, Hannibal, Charlemagne, Genghis Khan, Caesar, Mayan kings atop their stone temples.

RENEE: Caped crusaders.

BIGGAR: Warrior kings. I love the idea that there can be a decisive battle ... a series of physical actions on one field, on one night ... men writing history.

TRENT: In blood.

[Trent experiences a stab of bone pain.]

BIGGAR: *[as if Renee said it]* How else?

RENEE: Go on.

BIGGAR: And so, in a series of giant steps, I explored the breadth and depth of the last five hundred years and … and I feel that I am somehow a part of all that now. An inheritor, if you will, the sole speaker of a warrior tongue whispered back across these centuries. *[pause]* I see the larger pattern. I stand on the prow of time.

RENEE: That sounds … wonderful.

TRENT: Nurse, please, my morphine drip.

[Trent writhes in agony.]

BIGGAR: Given the above, there hasn't been much time for … for normal things.

RENEE: *[moving closer]* Such as?

BIGGAR: There has been a concomitant abjuration of … the pleasures of the flesh. Dr Johnson said, 'Whatever withdraws us from the power of our senses; whatever makes the past or the future predominate over the present, advances us in the dignity of thinking beings'.

RENEE: What about 'now'?

BIGGAR: What do you mean, 'now'?

RENEE: Now, as in, Be Here Now.

[Another stab of pain for Trent.]

BIGGAR: I'm afraid I – I have problems with that colloquialism. I mean, on one hand perhaps it's as John Dryden says –

RENEE: Stop quoting.

BIGGAR: I – I'm simply trying to tell you –

[She kisses him. He doesn't know how to respond.]

RENEE: The frog prince.

[She kisses him again. The kiss deepens. Trent stares out into the audience.]

[SOUND: *wind chimes.*]

[LIGHT *shift. Renee slips out of Biggar's embrace, leaving him there like a statue. Trent stares out into the audience. Renee moves around them, a curator in a museum.*]

RENEE: *[pre-recorded voice]* When you were in love you stood outside time. She drifted through your mind like a twist of smoke. She was in your thoughts at the oddest moments. She was the idea. She was the thing. She made you feel so powerful. She made you feel so lost and alone. She cast a spell on this mundane world and lifted it up into the light. For a time it was all so perfect, then she vanished into the ancient maze. Where did she go? *[Renee dons the mask and becomes Eve]*

In ancient days hunters believed women impregnated themselves with the wind or the sea.

So much love. So much fear. So much complexity. *[pause]* A man's mind is a lonely place. *[pause]* Siamese twins listening to the world through a membrane of skin. Everything so far away. *[to Biggar]* All the objects. *[to Trent]* All the ideas. So far, far away. *[pause]*

Who will live and who will die?

There must be a test. And a prize ... the future!

TRENT: Nurse. Nurse!

[LIGHTS *fade. A tight spot on Biggar's face. A tight spot on Trent's face.*]

[MUSIC *under: 'Walk Away, Renee' processional.*]

[Fade to black.]

[MUSIC *up: 'Walk Away, Renee' processional.]*

[FADE TO BLACK.]

[MUSIC *out, replaced by sounds of torture.]*

[LIGHT *flickers on slowly.]*

TRENT: Who is responsible for global warming? What are you doing about Third World debt? When will you feed the world's hungry? Why does military spending consume seventeen percent of the global economy? Where will ordinary people learn the truth about these issues if all our media outlets are controlled by a tiny handful of right-wing men?

[LIGHTS *up.]*

[Biggar is splayed on the upright bed/torture rack. He has been beaten to a pulp. Implements of torture are scattered about. Biggar comes around slowly.]

[Trent, wearing his torturer's hood, drops to one knee to catch his breath.]

TRENT: Answer me.

BIGGAR: *[groggy]* Must have food ... liquids ...

TRENT: Not until you come around to my way of thinking!

BIGGAR: Never.

[SOUND: *wind chimes.*]

[The sound makes Trent anxious. He scratches his crotch.]

TRENT: Nurse? Nurse! Come to me. I need you. Please.

BIGGAR: Strobing ... blood sugar ... *[whisper]* Tootsie Roll ... Tootsie Roll ...

[LIGHTS *blink out one by one.*]

[In a panic, Trent waves his palms in the gesture that previously shifted space-time. No effect. Biggar groans and struggles against his restraints.]

TRENT: Biggar!

BIGGAR: Who – who are you?

TRENT: You're having a hypoglycemic attack.

[Trent rummages in his pockets.]

BIGGAR: The bastard brother who wants to usurp my kingdom.

TRENT: This is my last section of Tootsie Roll, man. [LIGHTS *dim further]* Eat! There isn't much time.

BIGGAR: Torturer! Assassin!

[The LIGHTS *dim again. Biggar resists Trent.]*

TRENT: Eat this or die, brother!

BIGGAR: Never – never – never!

[Trent forces open Biggar's mouth.]

TRENT: Open your mouth! Open! Stick out your tongue! Now chew!

[Trent works Biggar's jaw. The sugar kicks in immediately and Biggar quiets.]

*[*LIGHTS *come back on one by one.]*

TRENT: That's it, Lionel. Bring it back around ... one quality at a time ...

BIGGAR: *[coming around]* Not an inch ...

[Trent helps Biggar regains his senses.]

TRENT: Sight ... sound ... touch ... smell ...

BIGGAR: *[sharpening up]* You stink.

TRENT: Atta boy.

[Biggar changes gears – he's enoying the Tootsie Roll enormously.]

[Drip. Drip. Drip.]

BIGGAR: The old hypoglycemic gambit. Your last morsel of food. Perfect. *[he finishes it]* So? Where do we go from here? The rubber hose? The thumbscrew? The glowing coat hanger?

TRENT: Excuse me?

BIGGAR: Yon black bag, dimwit. Menace me!

TRENT: I'm 'T', man! I am so tired.

BIGGAR: You lily-livered liberal lout. Retrieve a new implement of torture from the bag!

[Trent rummages in the bag and pulls out a speculum.]

TRENT: I don't get it.

BIGGAR: Have you no strategy? When you're ramping a man up to a fine point of agony, you want to be following a plan that he fully understands. The pain will increase in orderly increments until he comes around to your way of thinking. The trick, of course, is to convince the chap that you're actually a reluctant torturer – 'This hurts me more than it hurts you.' I found your performance rather wanting in that regard. You were enjoying yourself far too much.

TRENT: I – I take no pleasure in this, Biggar. It's a task that's been set for me by our captor ... I think ...

BIGGAR: That hood makes you look like a lawn jockey, by the way. Baboon Man.

TRENT: Do I have to kill you?

BIGGAR: Will I die for my beliefs at the hands of an inferior man? Gladly. Come and get it.

[Trent flogs Biggar.]

BIGGAR: Joined at the heart! If you kill me we both die!

[Trent stops the beating and pants. Drip. Drip. Drip.]

[Eve marches in.]

EVE: What is going on here?

[She jolts Trent.]

TRENT: I – I – I – I –

EVE: I'm watching on the closed circuit and it's making me crazy. Why are you listening to this?

TRENT: I – I'm sorry. The situation gets away from me.

EVE: It's a battle of wills, stupid! Your ideology against his.

BIGGAR: And the personal is political, right Mr Trent? *[to Eve]* One of his favourite slogans back in the old days.

EVE: You take this kind of crap? Nail him!

[Trent flogs Biggar.]

EVE: From the shoulder! Snap the wrist!

[Eve directs his swing from behind, like a golf pro.]

EVE: Shoulder – wrist. Shoulder – wrist.

[Trent really goes at it. Biggar makes that terrible gurgling sound and starts to convulse.]

EVE: There. That gurgling? You stop –

TRENT: This is so horrible. I'm a deeply non-violent person.

EVE: Snap out of it, Mr Trent. We've got work to do here. You don't want convulsions, very counterproductive. So you wait. You let him recover. As soon as he's refocused you ask him a simple question and if he doesn't bend to your will you nail him again. Tension – release. Tension – release. It's not rocket science.

BIGGAR: He has the IQ of a lobster.

TRENT: Shut up!

[He flogs Biggar in a rage. Eve pushes Trent aside, applies her thumb to Biggar's carotid artery.]

EVE: Excuse us for a moment ...

[In seconds Biggar is out cold.]

TRENT: Wow.

EVE: You are absolutely hopeless. This anger, anger, anger. A guy with his kind of domineering temperament sees it as a sign of weakness. He's already got way more power than you. Why are you giving him yours?

TRENT: I'm afraid of him.

[Drip. Drip. Drip.]

EVE: So am I. The planet is at risk. We've got to get rid of these father figures. These corrupt voices in our heads ...

It's country simple! This man thinks he owns us. Control your anger. Break down his thought processes. Induce regression. You are the parent figure.

TRENT: I – I'm the parent figure?

[Trent scratches his crotch.]

EVE: Stop scratching your crotch! I know, it's a real stretch but if you can't make that work … what are we doing here?

TRENT: Okay, okay, okay. I – I'll be the parent figure. No problemo.

EVE: Coercion leads to compliance. Pain is the vehicle. Remember the three D's of torture: Debility, Dependency, Dread.

TRENT: *[mumble]* Debility, dependency, dread. Debility, dependency … *[pause]* Do you have a pen I could borrow?

[She realizes what she's up against. She smiles.]

EVE: Burn out before you rust out. Oh, Mr Trent, what are we going to do with you?

[Drip. Drip. Drip. Trent is momentarily overcome.]

TRENT: Are you by any chance one of my nurses?

[Trent scratches his crotch.]

EVE: Stop scratching your crotch!

TRENT: What do you want from me?

EVE: Teach me how to lie.

[Biggar groans.]

BIGGAR: I – I'm sorry, even with reduced brain function, I couldn't help overhearing. You want museum-quality mendacity? Ask him about Renee.

EVE: *[to Trent]* And your response is?

TRENT: Look, ma, no anger.

[Trent flogs Biggar using the new and improved shoulder-wrist technique. He whistles while he works.]

[Biggar makes the gurgling sound.]

TRENT: Are you ready to encourage progressive opinions on your editorial pages?

BIGGAR: Never!

[Trent looks to her for approval.]

EVE: Better.

TRENT: Thanks. Thanks so much.

EVE: *[to Trent]* Don't let me down.

[She exits.]

TRENT: You can count on me. Hey, don't be a stranger ...

[Trent sags under the weight of his disease. He and Biggar are side by side.]

TRENT: I can't do this. I can't do this.

BIGGAR: Progressive opinions. You know what I love about owning a lot of newspapers? I don't have to encourage my editorial people to agree with me. They value their jobs. They want to catch my eye and move up the ladder. Public debate is reshaped, nature looks after the rest. Inevitably, certain points of view wither up and fall away. How are we doing here? Got a case of the wobblies?

TRENT: I am so lost. I – I have the distinct impression that I may already be dead.

BIGGAR: You certainly don't look well. Look at me, cut to ribbons, bit through the inside of my mouth a couple of times, cracked rib, numerous contusions. Still got my game face on. C'mon, Mr Trent, two scorpions in a bottle! I torture you! You torture me! We are bound! COME ON!

TRENT: *[to himself]* The fiends are upon me. If I'm dead then ... then this must be ... ahhh *[doubles up]* bone pain ...

BIGGAR: Indescribable pain, an utter absence of hope – sounds like the old burning lake to me.

TRENT: No, no, no Purgatory, please ... I mean, we're on a spiritual journey here ... there is a reason for this horror ... some kind of redemptive cleansing ... right?

BIGGAR: Why do you think you're entitled to a spiritual journey? Your parents were lapsed Catholics. You weren't even baptized.

TRENT: How do you know that?

BIGGAR: Oh, I know all sorts of things. Your father was a godless communist bastard.

TRENT: Not another word!

[Trent flogs him feebly.]

BIGGAR: Well, well – a new pressure point. *[schoolyard]* Godless communist bastard. Godless communist bastard. Godless communist bastard.

[Trent goes at him in a rage.]

BIGGAR: What are the three Ds of torture?

[The frenzy builds.]

TRENT: Shut up!

BIGGAR: Look at that rage! You really are terrified of me.

[Berserk flogging.]

TRENT: SHUTUPSHUTUPSHUTUP!

[Trent slumps to his knees, panting.]

TRENT: Please. I am a dead man … a spiritual journey …

[Biggar studies him. He chooses a gentler line of attack.]

BIGGAR: It really is a bit of a bind, isn't it? I mean, a non-violent man and here you are beating me to death. If I really am part of you, entwined around the very beating of your heart. Tension – release. Tension – release. Jealousy. Rage. Revenge. Well, talk about futility. One thing for sure, this young lady knows a thing or two about torture techniques.

TRENT: I get a strange feeling when I'm around her sometimes, as if we've met in some other life. For all I know she may be one of my nurses.

BIGGAR: I catch a whiff of Renee.

[Trent doubles up in pain.]

BIGGAR: *[laughing]* Code Red, Code Red, Mr Trent is having a bad hair day.

TRENT: I'm shattered, man. I – I don't know what to believe.

BIGGAR: Why don't you come and lie down beside me?

[Biggar makes a space for Trent.]

TRENT: Holy shit … my hospital bed.

[Trent lies down beside Biggar.]

BIGGAR: Welcome home.

TRENT: *[looks out at the audience]* The ceiling tiles …

BIGGAR: Your mind works like a salad spinner.

TRENT: I'm going to close my eyes and count to three. When I open them I'm going to be fully conscious and you are going to be gone.

[Trent closes his eyes. Drip. Drip. Drip. He opens them.]

BIGGAR: Seriously, let's talk about Renee. At bottom, I think that's what this is all about. Your life focused down to a single incident. The ancient battlefield where we put our principles to the test.

TRENT: I don't want to talk about Renee!

BIGGAR: Well, that's really too bad, because I do. She used to get drunk and call me at three o'clock in the morning, just to talk about you ...

TRENT: Nurse! NURSE!

BIGGAR: *[mocking him]* 'Nurse! Nurse!' You little crybaby!

[SOUND: echo of Al Green singing 'Hey-aaah, loooove isss ...']

[SOUND: hospital.]

[The nurse is a disembodied voice. Trent's sight line identifies the source as somewhere high above. Biggar sinks back into suspended animation when Trent ascends to full consciousness.]

TRENT: Soul pain. Morphine ... you promised to up my dosage ... please ... oh, please ...

NURSE: Calm down, Mr Trent.

TRENT: I have entered a strange netherworld. Hope dwindles ... help me ...

NURSE: Let's have a look at that drip unit.

[He lifts his shirt to reveal his morphine drip.]

TRENT: I – I think I should be on seven.

NURSE: You always think you should be on seven, Mr Trent.

[Slightly faster: Drip. Drip. Drip. He relaxes.]

NURSE: You were asleep all morning. I didn't want to wake you. How are we doing?

TRENT: Not so good. I get trapped in these nightmarish scenarios, a monster squeezing my heart, so much pain and suffering.

NURSE: Calm your mind ... out of this muck grows the lotus flower. Have you been listening to your tapes?

TRENT: Yes, the lotus flower, yes, yes, yes. *[pause]* How long will I hover like this?

NURSE: There are things we can't know. Life is all about transformation, Mr Trent. To love and be loved, to forgive and be forgiven, to be known. These are the only things that matter.

TRENT: Transformation, yes. To be known, yes. A spiritual journey, yes, yes, yes.

[Drip. Drip. Drip.]

TRENT: *[drifting off]* Could you put on a tape for me, darling? Something soothing. It's been a long day. My brain is totally fried.

NURSE: Crickets and hoot owls?

TRENT: Zamfir.

[SOUND: generic Zamfir. Drip. Drip. Drip. Trent lies back into the music and digs at his crotch.]

NURSE: Don't do that, Mr Trent. You have a fungal infection. We're trying to clean it up.

TRENT: You are the most beautiful woman. We have met before, I promise you. That twinkle in your eye.

NURSE: Yes we have, Mr Trent. I'm on the ward every afternoon.

TRENT: What's your name again?

NURSE: Eve.

TRENT: Eve, of course, I knew that. *[memorizing it]* Eve, Eve, Eve. *[pause]* I have a crazy idea, Eve. You know those visualization exercises we've been doing?

NURSE: The sunset meditations?

TRENT: *[whisper]* Shh. Top secret. We use those hypnosis techniques to escape from this dump. I need one of those columns of energy you were talking about.

NURSE: A gate in time.

TRENT: Exactly, a soft-focus spiritual journey – the seashore, the seagulls, a white picket fence with a gate, a bower of lilacs, you know the drill – you lay out the scenario and give me a massive hit of morphine. I slip across the border and we walk away together ... hey, it's a theory.

NURSE: All the nurses talk about your theories, Mr Trent. You're quite the charmer.

TRENT: *[reminding himself]* And your name is Eve.

NURSE: Very good, Mr Trent.

TRENT: *[coming on]* Eve, have I told you about my career in journalism?

NURSE: You fought for the common good. You believed in change and becoming.

TRENT: I had a pretty good kick at the old can, Eve. I was the little guy with the big hatpin, gutter of page three every Tuesday. Still got a few rounds left in me. So, how about it? You deploy the visualization, I OD on the good stuff, we walk on rose petals, I stay with you, I protect you, we are happy forever after, world without end, amen ... whaddya say, kiddo?

NURSE: You are such a flirt, Mr Trent. I've got to finish my rounds.

TRENT: Please, don't go, take my hand, just for a minute. *[pause]* I am so afraid.

[He closes his eyes and holds out his hand. Eve enters from behind.]

NURSE: I was in here earlier today. You'd drifted off. You were talking about Renee again ...

[SOUND: *the Zamfir distorts.]*

EVE: Surprise, surprise! It was only me. *[mock nurse]* How are we feeling today, Mr Trent?

TRENT: Not so hot.

EVE: This isn't working out. You were going to be the parent figure, remember? Instead of that you park our friend on death's doorstep and wander off, to do what? Did I hear right? Were you actually trying to get laid?

[Drip. Drip. Drip.]

TRENT: It was a long shot. *[he shrinks under her gaze]* I – I was looking for a way out.

EVE: *[disgust]* One of those 'soft-focus spiritual journeys' with a side order of lotus flowers. What happened to bringing him around to your way of thinking? Look at me!

TRENT: I – I'm a desperate man. I seek an end to this suffering.

EVE: Don't talk to me about suffering, okay? I do not need this. I really do not need this. You are making me crazy.

TRENT: I – I'm sorry I tried to escape. I'll never, ever do it again. I promise.

EVE: You make promises, then you run away. I mean, we're inside your head, right? I'm here! I'm your creation! Why do you keep running away? *[pause]* I'm waiting for the penny to drop. When are you going to recognize me? When are you going to call me by my name?

TRENT: I – I get confused. You terrify me.

EVE: What if I'm the only one who can release you from this suffering?

[Drip. Drip. Drip.]

TRENT: Who are you?

[Drip. Drip. Drip.]

EVE: My name is Eve. I was born in Ingonish in a little cottage by the sea ...

[SOUND: wind chimes.]

TRENT: *[doubling up]* I'm sorry. This pain ...

EVE: Enough with the tortured soul shit, okay? You think you're in pain? You have no idea. I watched my mother drink herself to death. Sometimes Renee didn't make it home at night. I'd wake up in a ghost house. Empty fields. No neighbours for miles. I was this tall. Can't you see her in my eyes? Can't you hear yourself in my voice? *[whisper]* Hi, Dad ... can I come in ... or are you on your way out?

[It's too much. He covers his face.]

TRENT: Dear God, from the bottom of my soul I thank you for this. I – I'm sorry that I tried to escape from my suffering. The pain is not a problem now. I promise if you keep me on this plane of being I will make a full and complete atonement for all my sins. I promise I will stay with this young woman. We'll talk and laugh and walk on rose petals in the afternoon light. Please, please, please, God, keep me here until this work is done. I promise you I will never let her down.

EVE: You don't even believe in God.

TRENT: Can't a guy turn over a new leaf?

EVE: As if. You are sooo not ready for atonement. I mean, look at this little battlefield you've arranged for yourself.

[She indicates Biggar. He goes into spasms and convulsions – that horrible gurgle.]

EVE: Don't just stand there, do something! He's swallowing his tongue!

[Trent controls Biggar. He goes limp. She checks his eyes.]

EVE: Spontaneous convulsions. I don't know how much more of this he can take.

TRENT: Couldn't we just, you know, wander off and have cup of decaf somewhere? Just the two of us ... there are so many things I want to say to you ...

EVE: Joined at the heart. If he dies, where does that leave you? Or is that too sticky a theoretical proposition?

TRENT: I want to be with you. I want to be known by you. Just tell me what to do.

EVE: I'll tell you one thing. I hate the anger you gave me. If it eats me alive I'll fail ... just like you. *[pause]* What did we need those old ice caps for, anyway?

TRENT: We're on the same team! I want the world to win.

EVE: *[indicating Biggar]* Then make peace with your demons. It's our only hope.

TRENT: Peace with the demons, yes, yes, yes. I'll get right on it.

[Biggar makes the horrible gargling sound.]

EVE: *[exiting]* There's that sound again.

BIGGAR: *[panting]* Food, please ... I perish.

[Hypoglycemia is coming on strong.]

TRENT: You inhaled the last piece of Tootsie Roll, man.

BIGGAR: I'll suck the lining of your pocket.

[Biggar is in a full-on diabetic seizure, thrashing and gargling and trying to swallow his own tongue. Trent locks his arms and legs around him.]

TRENT: Okay, okay, okay. I got you, Big Guy.

[He stuffs candy in Biggar's mouth.]

TRENT: I – I was holding out on you. I had a stash of gummi bears.

BIGGAR: Gummi-gummi-gummi ...

[He eats. Trent gets his head back together, figuring a sidelong strategy.]

TRENT: I had a little chat with our captor. Quite the gal.

BIGGAR: *[eating]* ... very, very capable young woman ... good solid plan ... leave us alone ... watch us on the closed circuit ... see what develops ... top-notch stuff ...

[Trent waves and smiles, just in case there's a hidden camera in the room.]

TRENT: *[secret]* Who do you think she is? I get this blur sometimes. You know, on one level she's an eco-terrorist, she's also a bit like one of my nurses ... and then there's that whiff of Renee you mentioned ... a minute ago she had me convinced she was Renee's daughter.

BIGGAR: The morphine drip takes you strange places, Mr Trent.

TRENT: Yeah, that must be it. *[pause]* You know what? I think you should try some.

BIGGAR: I'm not the morphine type.

TRENT: C'mon, c'mon, c'mon, Big Guy, you're beaten to shit, that's what this stuff is for.

BIGGAR: I'm feeling fit now. Let's get back to the old torture rack.

TRENT: No more torture. I want us to make peace.

BIGGAR: How can there be peace between us? We have no common ground.

TRENT: Excuse me? We've got some 'fessing up to do, Big Guy. C'mon, one sundowner, what can it hurt? Nurse? Nurse? Get this gentleman a few grains of your finest Afghani schmeckety-schmeck. Thank you, darling. Thank you so very much. And that Zamfir tape? Thanks. The nurses all love me.

BIGGAR: You're a fog of charm and ambience.

[They laugh together.]

TRENT: See? Let the pressure off. We're just a couple of guys doing heroin.

*[*MUSIC *under: Zamfir.]*

TRENT: Go like this –

[Trent shows Biggar how to pump his forearm. An injection gun flies in.]

TRENT: *[to the invisible nurse]* Thanks, darling.

[Trent injects Biggar.]

BIGGAR: Ah, I see. Lure me into bed. Get me stoned.

[Trent injects himself.]

TRENT: Hey, Lionel, erase those pesky barriers, here comes the peace train, man ... wait for it ...

*[*MUSIC *up: distorted Zamfir, a mournful Mississippi blues train.]*

[Biggar sags as the morphine hits.]

BIGGAR: So ... this is it ... the infamous heroin high.

TRENT: Peace in a syringe. The opiate of hope for no-hopers the world over. Look at those ceiling tiles, Big Guy. How's that for an effect?

BIGGAR: Holy doodle.

TRENT: Okay, the journey to peace, one stepping stone at a time. Peace is built on understanding and forgiveness. You and I need to see each other in a new way. Here's where I'm at: I lie in this bed and stare at those acoustic tiles and I just, you know, I review the data. I can tell you there's not much to hold onto, all the public and private identities fall away as the story is further simplified – unnecessary, unnecessary, irrelevant – right down to the nub of the very nub.

BIGGAR: *[very stoned]* I love the nub.

TRENT: What is it for you?

BIGGAR: The legacy. The whorl of my thumbprint in time.

TRENT: Right on.

BIGGAR: What else is there?

TRENT: That essence left on the finest of the fine screens where the gods harvest our souls.

[Drip. Drip. Drip. They both put thumbprints in the air. They're enjoying themselves.]

BIGGAR: What is your essence? Paint me a picture.

TRENT: A man swan dives across an abyss. Is he falling or flying? It doesn't matter. He's grinning like a fool. It has nothing to do with bravery. It's a kind of blind stupidity … fuelled by a child's hope.

BIGGAR: I know the feeling, a kind of giddy dread, up so high on the prow of time.

TRENT: There was no big plan, right?

BIGGAR: None whatever. Ad hoc-ery right the way through.

TRENT: No big picture, we were making it up as we went along.

BIGGAR: It was all dancing.

TRENT: Yeah, it was dancing …

[Biggar does a snippet of the dirty dance for Trent's amusement. They both chuckle.]

TRENT: Wouldn't it be great if it all … finally … meant something?

BIGGAR: It would be so great.

[Pause. A bonding moment for them. Trent takes Biggar's hand.]

TRENT: I guess we'd have to agree to disagree about precisely what that final meaning might be.

[He tucks into Biggar, spooning.]

BIGGAR: Bloodied boxers embracing after a title bout.

TRENT: We'll never see eye to eye.

BIGGAR: *[sings]* You say tomato …

[They dance cheek to cheek.]

TRENT: And a grand old time was had by one and all ...

[They laugh and snuggle together.]

TRENT: This is so incredible. You are curing my cancer, man. There's love coursing through your body into my body and I – I can feel it shrinking my tumours. I'm serious, I can feel it! *[pause]* We're standing outside our rage.

BIGGAR: I think not.

[Biggar disentangles himself from Trent.]

TRENT: *[hurt]* Why?

BIGGAR: I'm a realist, remember? We are men. We want the ten thousand small advantages. Inevitably there will be cycles of revenge and destruction.

TRENT: Unless we stop it.

BIGGAR: Why should I forgive you for defaming my sexual performance in your newspaper in 1968?

TRENT: Why should I forgive you for what your mother did to my father?

BIGGAR: I know the story. The man had a heart attack on a picket line.

TRENT: Her scabs were beating the strikers with pool cues.

BIGGAR: Was he hit?

TRENT: No.

BIGGAR: Well, then, what's your point? The people who owned the mine wanted to run it. Is there something wrong with that?

TRENT: I've got this marketing idea for my book – your face on a urinal puck.

[Drip. Drip. Drip.]

TRENT: Thank God she came along ...

BIGGAR: She?

TRENT: My daughter. That's who our captor is, Big Guy, you might as well digest that fact. My long-lost daughter – a warrior-goddess come to me in the garment of my final moments on this plane of being.

BIGGAR: Lord have mercy.

TRENT: That young woman is the thumbprint of my existence in this world ... the dharma wheel turns.

BIGGAR: Ah, the dreaded dharma wheel. Bullshit detectors ON.

TRENT: She knows that I know, and I know that she knows I know. We haven't really gotten down to talking about it yet –

BIGGAR: Of course not, how could you? 'So, you're the man who wanted to have me aborted.'

TRENT: *[overriding him]* It's one of those tacit things ... you can't jump straight to tenderness, there are gonna be some bumps. Given our history.

*[*SOUND: *wind chimes.]*

TRENT: I gave Renee those wind chimes, by the way. She probably didn't tell you that when she hung them on the porch of that cozy little cottage in Ingonish. And every time she heard them ...

BIGGAR: Dream on.

TRENT: *[on his own track]* I – I always pictured a boy child. You know, my son, my legacy. That was such a total failure of imagination. I mean, this gal is dynamite. Eco-terrorism. She's got the big picture in focus, man! There are still kids out there who are willing to go to the barricades. That makes me so proud ... so happy. What did I do to deserve such a beautiful kid? *[pause, points]* Is that a star or a planet?

*[*SOUND: *wind chimes.]*

BIGGAR: That is the porch light on my grandfather's saltbox in Ingonish. Renee's inside right now, she's sitting in the kitchen drinking a tumbler of rye and ginger. A man she hardly knows is sitting across from her in his underwear. His tow truck is parked on the front lawn. Twenty minutes ago they were having wild sex on a waterbed in the living room. Her little girl is in the back bedroom trying to watch cartoons. *[pause]* It wasn't your child, by the way. That's a very nice narrative twist but that's not at all how it goes.

TRENT: Hey, Lionel, c'mon, you know and I know ...

[He mimes a limp dick.]

BIGGAR: Renee instructed me in the joys of carnality.

TRENT: Hey, hey, hey, I sent her to you. She was on a political errand, Big Guy. She told me everything that happened. Back to your problem with the noodle – you should get checked out, man. There's a pill now.

BIGGAR: Biological paternity is hardly the point. I gave the child sanction. I wrote the cheques that provided for her material well-being. The best private schools. Some rather posh travel to foreign trouble spots so she could see for herself the way this world works. I was shaping her thinking. All of this achieved by me at a distance, mind you. Renee was a lost cause by then. She'd phone me drunk at three o'clock in the morning, trying to make it right. I put her daughter through university. She graduated summa cum laude from Brown and received a Fulbright Scholarship. She is currently a fellow at the Fraser Institute in Vancouver. She's doing a study of foreign-aid scandals in the Third World. Little-known fact: most of what we give goes to waste.

TRENT: No way, man. No daughter of mine would ever do that.

BIGGAR: Well, that's what she's doing. That's the light in her office. She's blazing away at her computer, taking the piss out of the hand-wringing liberal nitwits who run Operation Lifeline Sudan or the World Food Program. Save the world. Greenhouse gases. Carbon sinks. What a load of bollocks. She's mine!

TRENT: Bullshit!

BIGGAR: I wrote the cheques!

TRENT: She was just here talking to me, man. As soon as I make my peace with you she's coming back and we're headed off for a leisurely lunch in some brand new never-never.

BIGGAR: There'll be no peace between us.

TRENT: We're inside my head, Gumby! You don't dictate reality in this jurisdiction.

BIGGAR: Is that so? Well, c'mon then, you snivelling socialist snot rag, show me your stuff! You want peace? Beat it into my head! C'MON!

[Trent is back on his feet. He flogs Biggar in a frenzy.]

TRENT: PEACE! NOW! PEACE! NOW! PEACE! NOW!

[Trent falls to his knees. Both men are panting with pain.]

BIGGAR: Good stuff ... you've earned your keep ... I'll tell you a little story.

[Drip. Drip. Drip.]

BIGGAR: Renee fell down the basement stairs and cracked her head open on the corner of a filing cabinet full of my grandfather's papers. She lay there all night in a pool of blood. Guess who found her?

[Drip. Drip. Drip.]

BIGGAR: Early the next morning, her eight-year-old daughter tiptoed downstairs in her pyjamas: *[singsong]* 'Mummy,

Mummy, Mummy, where are you hiding? You can't hide from me. I'm gonna find you.'

[Drip. Drip. Drip.]

BIGGAR: ... and, of course, Evie did.

[Trent falls to his knees. Biggar is pleased as punch.]

BIGGAR: Ahh, you see? I take your best shot and come right back at you. I've told you something now. Have you got a cozy spot for it in your moral framework?

TRENT: Fuck, man, don't you ever stop?

BIGGAR: Don't do the crime if you can't do the time, Mr Trent. We are here on the shore of the burning lake. Get some sulfur up your nose! *[secret]* I particularly loved that soft skin at the nape of Renee's neck.

[Trent is on his back, writhing in pain.]

TRENT: Nurse. Nurse!

BIGGAR: Wrong rabbit hole, Mr Trent. I understand the blur, by the way. That nurse does look a little bit like Renee ...

TRENT: You took Renee off on your little power trip. She followed your advice and –

BIGGAR: *[interrupting]* She loved me. I tried to save her. I failed because you had infected her with your libertine ideas.

TRENT: Your view of history is so utterly distorted by self-interest. You have no idea what really went down in the sixties, the energy, the commitment. How could you?

You were tooling around in your Bentley. It was a crusade, man, we were at the barricades saving the world.

BIGGAR: Better put, you were trying to steal it.

TRENT: Smash and grab at midnight, Big Guy. That's how we took you down, down, DOWN!

[MUSIC up: Al Green, 'Love and Happiness']

[LIGHT shift to indicate a fire. Trent grooves to the music, taunting Biggar with his dance. Renee dances into the light.]

TRENT: I know I'm pushing you. I see the person you can be. I don't want you stuck in some stupid little life with marigolds all in a row. It's up to us to visualize the future. We're going to live in that shining hour – hope! meaning! – world without end, amen.

RENEE: As long as I don't have to call this guy up and lie.

TRENT: You're dancing like a Hutterite. Bend your knees a little.

RENEE: Shut up.

[He embraces her. They sway to the music.]

RENEE: Show me the future. Ten years from now. Where am I?

TRENT: No, you go. You and me somewhere. Paint me a picture.

[Renee thinks for a moment.]

RENEE: Okay. We live in this little white bungalow in ... um ... Bella Coola.

TRENT: Bella Coola?

RENEE: Never been there, love the sound – *[Italian]* Bella Coola.

TRENT: I'll be in the pub playing darts with the unemployed fishermen. *[drunk]* Bella Coola.

RENEE: Uh-uh. My story. You hardly drink at all. In fact I think you quit. You're writing a big book about something or other.

TRENT: Fair enough.

RENEE: I'm a registered nurse. *[off his look]* Somebody's got to buy the groceries. We live in a little house on this rocky point with waves crashing in –

TRENT: An abandoned lighthouse. Round rooms. Très cool.

RENEE: Okay, and there's this huge round kitchen with a fieldstone fireplace set in the wall ...

TRENT: Also round.

RENEE: On a wild day, spray hammers at the door. It sounds like a giant trying to get in. Your writing room, also round, is way up top, where the light used to be. You stand up there in your little glass capsule, the booming surf, the wind ...

TRENT: *[laughing]* And I haven't got a clue what the hell I'm doing! Where are the people? What are the issues? Help me out here.

RENEE: Right off the kitchen is the baby's room, also round – *[off his look]* What?

TRENT: The way you zap me with those eyes. You are so beautiful.

RENEE: So you say.

TRENT: I see hope.

[He kisses her.]

TRENT: Maybe you're not up for this guerilla journalism thing. That's cool, too.

RENEE: I don't know ... cold-calling some guy I don't know and telling him a bunch of lies.

TRENT: It's called dropping your pants for the cause.

RENEE: What if everybody lied? What kind of world would it be?

TRENT: A world very much like this one. We live in a swamp of lies and nobody is talking about it. Our political system is arranged to suit the needs of a tiny plutocratic elite. This guy Biggar thinks he can buy an election. Over my dead body.

RENEE: Why does everything turn into a fight for you?

TRENT: I grew up on this stuff. *[pause]* I never told you about my old man. A hard-core, fire-breathing commie bastard. He dropped dead before I really got to know him. He was a major shit disturber in the coal miners' union, always in and out of jail. I wouldn't see him for months, then he'd make bail and waltz in the door some morning with tall tales about what they tried to do to me and what I did to them. I sat there at the kitchen table listening to him talk about the big issues … an old-time warrior. One of the leaders of our tribe.

RENEE: What tribe?

TRENT: We the people. *[pause]* It doesn't matter. What matters is that I've found you and we're on this journey together.

RENEE: A man with a plan.

TRENT: Change the world, one person at a time.

[He kisses her.]

RENEE: I am who I am, Trent.

TRENT: I love you so much.

[They start to grind.]

TRENT: There. Feel the power? That's who we are …

[MUSIC *up.]*

[LIGHT *shift. Firelight builds to burning-lake levels as the dirty dance turns into raunchy sex.]*

[Sexual panting builds in intensity and turns into the earthquake sound cue from Act One. Lightning flash. Crash of thunder. Sexual panting turns into horrible gasping. LIGHTS *snap to torture cell levels. Biggar is in convulsions again. Trent instinctively moves to help him.]*

TRENT: Biggar! Biggar! Wait! You can't die, I'm not finished changing you yet!

[Trent can't believe it. He takes Biggar's pulse. Listens for breathing. It sinks in – Biggar's dead. He looks closer. He touches Biggar's face with his finger, monkey-like. Trent lies down beside Biggar. He's ready to die. Biggar rolls and clamps Trent around the ankle.]

BIGGAR: Mr Crocodile lay on the bottom and watched Mr Bush Pig going down for the third time ... those little pink trotters ...

[Biggar is working his way up Trent's leg.]

BIGGAR: Drag him down to the green river! Wedge him under a log and let the water soften him up!

[He has his chain wrapped around Trent's neck. They fall back onto the bed.]

BIGGAR: One Mississippi – time for some obedience training, Mr Trent. Two Mississippi – it's called grace under pressure. It's called doing the right thing. Three Mississippi – watch closely, Mr Trent, I'll show you how a real gentleman comports himself.

[Trent makes the gargling sound. Renee appears in the light.]

BIGGAR: *[lost in his anecdote]* Battle of Copenhagen, the ships side by side, blasting away at each other with cannonball and chain – boom-boom-boom! Masts exploding! The decks of Lord Nelson's crippled vessel slippery with the best English blood! Gravely wounded men crying out for their mothers –

TRENT: *[whisper]* Psst. Renee.

[She pretends not to notice him.]

BIGGAR: One of Lord Nelson's signal officers came to the quarterdeck with an urgent message: 'The Admiral has run up the signal flag ordering disengagement with the enemy' –

TRENT: *[whisper, to Renee]* This is a bad idea. Go home to me.

BIGGAR: – and he held the spyglass up to his blind eye, observed the Admiral's ship, and said the four most famous words in the history of the Royal Navy: 'I see no flag'. *[laughs]* Talk about warrior kings! Outmanœuvre the Russians! Close with the French! Why don't you come and lie here by me on the divan?

TRENT: *[whisper]* Don't!

[Renee lies down. Trent is in the middle. The Biggar–Renee scenes play across him.]

RENEE: I really shouldn't be doing this. *[to Trent]* It was the way he told his story.

TRENT: *[whisper]* Politics as foreplay.

RENEE: *[whisper]* Exactly your game.

BIGGAR: Before we go any further, I have a question. Was there something going on between you and that obnoxious houseman at the club tonight? I don't know. I was aware of this rather odd ... frisson.

TRENT: *[whisper]* If he only knew.

BIGGAR: *[on his own track]* My mother used to say, 'Are they from our tribe?' One of those expressions that covered an enormous range of issues, from skin colour to the wearing of diamond pinky rings. My point is, you work on that loathsome newspaper – if you're really in league with that bunch – there can be no real intimacy between us.

RENEE: *[to Biggar]* What can I tell you about Trent? When he's sober he wants to save the world. When he's drunk he falls into bed with women he hardly knows.

TRENT: *[whisper]* Time out.

BIGGAR: And you, perhaps, are one of those unfortunate individuals?

RENEE: Me, oh, heavens no, what a thought! *[to Trent]* The first lie. Can you feel the ripples?

BIGGAR: You had some questions for me. We never got around to them.

RENEE: I want to understand the way you think, Lionel.

BIGGAR: Usually in well-punctuated paragraphs. Gotcha!

[He embraces her. Trent is the ham in the sandwich.]

TRENT: *[whisper]* You should have slapped his face.

RENEE: *[whisper]* He was telling me all about his family.

BIGGAR: ... they called him the King of Carbon! He drove his collieries out under the Atlantic.

[He pulls her closer and grinds his hips against Trent.]

BIGGAR: Drove and drove and drove again his great, gleaming shaft into that ancient Precambrian bedrock. The piston of progress! He was pushing the engineering principles of his day and there were of course some catastrophes ...

[Biggar pulls Renee closer still. Trent is really squashed now.]

TRENT: *[muffled]* Help! I can't breathe!

[But it's too late. Biggar is grinding in earnest now.]

BIGGAR: *[gruff]* Fondle the staff of my manhood.

TRENT: *[muffled]* Run!

RENEE: I don't think I'd better, Lionel.

[They dry hump awkwardly with Trent caught in the middle. He surfaces from time to time like a drowning swimmer caught in raging surf. Biggar fakes an orgasm.]

BIGGAR:Yes, oh, yes … yes indeed, yes … oh, most assuredly yes-yes-YES!

[He and Renee roll apart.]

BIGGAR: *[panting]* Well, well, wasn't that just the berries.

TRENT: *[panting whisper]* You never told me he kept his pants on.

RENEE: *[whisper]* There are a lot of things I never told you.

TRENT: *[whisper]* Did he have an orgasm?

RENEE: Did you come, Lionel?

BIGGAR: *[checks his crotch]* I – I'm not sure.

RENEE: That means you didn't.

BIGGAR: Yes, well, a man's reach must exceed his ... and so on ...

[Biggar slips into uncomfortable silence.]

TRENT: *[whisper]* If I'd known that, I'd have had a completely different mental picture. A dog humping a sofa leg.

BIGGAR: *[on his own track]* I was just recalling some reading I did on the subject, Renee. Biomechanically speaking, a penis is akin to an earthworm or a squid tentacle –

RENEE: It's all right, Lionel. You don't have to apologize.

TRENT: *[British waiter]* Hello, my name is Charles, I'll be your penis this evening. *[pause]* If he wasn't the father why did you tell him you were pregnant?

*[*LIGHT *shift. Renee and Biggar move away from Trent. Renee looks at Biggar. She's been crying, having just told him about her pregnancy.]*

RENEE: I – I don't know why I wanted you to know. I just did.

BIGGAR: It's not as if ...

RENEE: Of course not.

BIGGAR: Well, I'm honoured that you've chosen to take me into your confidence. I wasn't sure of our footing these last few weeks, I mean, after there was no response to my notes.

RENEE: What notes?

TRENT: *[whisper]* I'm sorry. I couldn't help myself.

BIGGAR: Ah, just as well. They were rather florid.

[Pause. Trent moves away.]

BIGGAR: If I might ask, who is the father?

RENEE: Remember Trent?

TRENT: *[whisper]* Who was I to parent a child? My life was a shambles. I had the jeans I was wearing, two sweatshirts and a carton of books. I'd have had to get a job stacking apples in a grocery store.

RENEE: *[whisper]* I did that job, and a lot like it.

BIGGAR: That little worm who wrote the article defaming me? *[she nods, Biggar does the emotional math]* And you … and he … *[pause, she nods]* … that's where he got the information for … I would be fibbing if I said the thought hadn't occurred to me. I mean, who else could have … ?

RENEE: Trent used me to get at you. I've been sick about it ever since.

TRENT: *[whisper, his own cancer]* A single grain of evil.

RENEE: If you can forgive me, I'll go.

BIGGAR: Of course I forgive you. But surely my forgiveness is of only minor consequence, Renee, given the other matters you must attend to. What is your plan?

RENEE: I'm in such a mess … I'm sorry, I promised I wouldn't cry and here I am looking like a complete idiot. I need five hundred dollars. That's what I need. Enough money to get out of here … I'm sorry, I shouldn't have come. I can't go home. My parents would kill me. I don't know which way to turn …

BIGGAR: What does your friend have to say about it?

[LIGHT *shift. Renee leaves Biggar and moves to Trent.*]

RENEE: He's a human being, Trent. You have no right to defame him like this.

TRENT: He's running for public office. The personal is political.

RENEE: He told me these things in confidence.

TRENT: You want the hard truth? He told you the personal stuff to get into your pants. It's what men do when they're seriously on the make: 'Oh, poor me, look at these wounds'.

RENEE: It's what you do.

[Pause.]

TRENT: What was he like in the sack? You never told me.

[Pause.]

TRENT: You actually went to bed with him?

RENEE: How many times do I have to tell you? We didn't have sex.

TRENT: I don't believe you. *[pause]* You slut.

RENEE: You really are a case.

TRENT: I'm going with it.

RENEE: Gutter journalism.

TRENT: Journalists belong in the gutter because that is where the ruling classes throw their filthy secrets!

RENEE: I won't let you do this!

TRENT: You're out of your depth here, okay? This has nothing to do with growing up on a fucking Christmas tree farm.

RENEE: Trent –

TRENT: My father spent his life crusading against these bastards! He dropped dead of a heart attack on a picket line! Don't tell me what I'm allowed to write!

RENEE: I don't want to see you again. I'll leave your stuff in the office.

[Pause.]

TRENT: And I thought I could trust you.

[Pause.]

RENEE: I don't even know who you are, Trent. *[pause]* And I missed my period.

[Pause.]

TRENT: Whoa.

RENEE: Is that all you can say?

[LIGHT *shift.*]

BIGGAR: I'll bite out the bastard's tongue.

[Renee regains herself.]

RENEE: I never meant to hurt you, Lionel.

BIGGAR: This baby will need a father.

TRENT: *[whisper]* Don't listen.

RENEE: That's not why I came –

TRENT: *[whisper]* He's looking for a way to get at me.

BIGGAR: I'm at my best in a crisis, Renee.

TRENT: *[whisper]* This is not your destiny calling.

BIGGAR: Lord Nelson, your presence is required on the quarterdeck.

TRENT: *[whisper]* It wasn't exactly a black and white situation. You were on the pill. We'd been involved for exactly six weeks. You fooled around with a guy I hated. You got pregnant. I didn't want you to ruin your life.

BIGGAR: Money solves problems. That is precisely why it is worth having.

RENEE: All I need is five hundred dollars.

BIGGAR: This scoundrel thinks he can play fast and loose with the rules that bind our social order. We'll have none of it. I have a heart, too. I won't see you left like this. I shall set this world to rights.

RENEE: I'll pay you back as soon as I can.

TRENT: *[whisper]* Please, one more chance. The lighthouse in Bella Coola.

RENEE: *[whisper]* I'm hardly even here, Trent. I'm a twist of smoke. The memory of a memory.

BIGGAR: Five hundred dollars will solve your short-term problem. What about the long term? I have the financial means to imagine anything I want, Renee, and by imagining things I make them true.

TRENT: *[whisper]* I'll work in a grocery store. I'll pump gas. We'll walk on rose petals.

BIGGAR: I will amply provide for your material well-being.

RENEE: I'd better go.

BIGGAR: Wait! My grandfather left me a small fishing lodge in Ingonish. Rustic cabins scattered along a rather lovely stretch of rocky shore. You could go there and see this matter through to a happy conclusion. Do you like the seashore?

[Pause.]

RENEE: Yes, I do.

BIGGAR: Well then, let's not hear another word about it. I'll let my groundsman in Cape Breton know you're on the way –

RENEE: But –

[He covers her mouth.]

BIGGAR: I take away all your choices. You've never felt so free.

TRENT: *[whisper]* Soul pain! Nurse!

[Trent lies down in agony.]

EVE: *[whisper]* You told her, 'I don't care who the father is. This was a stupid accident'. I've been through it, okay? A couple of times. It's a horrendous afternoon with your knees in the air. You ran out of words. She was crying. And then you left. *[pause]* You never even said goodbye. I didn't understand that. I was your kid, how could you not care?

[She moves off.]

EVE: I imagine her last thought at the bottom of those stairs ... a lighthouse on the rock ... round rooms ... *[saying ciao]* Bella Coola ...

[Eve and Biggar exit into darkness.]

TRENT: Soul pain ... nurse ...

[LIGHT shift. Trent his alone on his catafalque as it tilts into the upright position.]

TRENT: The ceiling tiles ... the small frame of these final moments ... I lie here and wonder: What remains on the finest of the fine screens ... ?

[Trent dies. Pause. Trent stands.]

The chains of thought and feeling that bound me to this world let go one by one ... the gates of time open wide ... I float free in the ancient trance ...

[He moves.]

I walk with Mayan kings and talk of bankrupt ideologies. The forest is so thick that you enter their ruined city unaware. Then green shadows deepen, and looking up through the canopy of leaves you see a stone tower blazing in the sun. The buildings might be cliffs, except that here is a stairway smothered in roots, a mossy statue, a crumbling inscription to some vanished god. The Mayans succumbed to environmental collapse, too, the whole thing went to hell in less than a hundred years, the end coming in a final spasm of economic and social chaos. Faced with bad news, the response of the mighty was to build higher pyramids. Thus, this extravagant flowering on the eve of total collapse, these towers, these tombs, the whorl of this thumbprint in time. The earth is littered with dead civilizations stranded in deserts of their own making.

I have lived inside the story of my century, watching us blunder along, this guy in charge, that guy, left, right, left, right, hut-hut-hut – the march of the lemmings. And where did all of that get us? At the end of my days the three richest men in the world have a net worth equal to the forty-eight poorest countries! The number living in abject poverty is equal to the entire population of the world a hundred years ago! And the leader of the world's greatest democracy believes that poverty is not caused by a lack of money, it's caused by a lack of moral values on behalf of the poor. Once again, it's all their fault.

The crude glory of Late Capitalism. The winners want to keep on winning. They'll win and win right down to the last molecule of air – they'll suck it from the lungs of a dying child and hold it in, watching while the last light fades on this world. 'I'm the king of the castle. You're the dirty rascal.'

What is to be done? How do you stop a freight train with a feather? Those dots down there are human beings. Mankind in its billions. Don't talk to me about the salvations of technology. Eighty percent of the people on this earth have never used a telephone. And don't expect answers from the throne room. The rule of the many by the few has turned into a cruel casino game. A permanent circus of stupefying distractions.

Thank God for television, our font of truth at the end of each day. *[flips remote control]* Oh boy, a nature show! *[mellow announcer]* The Great Barrier Reef is older and bigger than anything human beings have ever made. *[a tycoon on the phone]* Oh yeah, the corals. I'll get to it right after lunch.

I mean, does anyone here qualify as an adult?

I was a satirist, a little man with a big hatpin separating the emperor from his new clothes. I attacked hypocrisy and lies and took the truth for granted. The contents of my own life remained a mystery to me. So much complexity. So much debility, dependency and dread. *[pause]* I was so loyal to my despair. It was a form of cowardice. There will be no dignified final exit for me, no graceful back door out of this story. I am my own last victim, these words caught on the barbed hook of my thinking, these last storms in my head.

I must let go of it all ... and look elsewhere ... what is outside the frame of this thinking?

In the end there is nothing left but the simple language of the heart. By seeing less ... I see more ... the kingdom within ...

A stretch of rocky shore ... a lighthouse ... a white brushstroke on a sea of cobalt blue ... round rooms ... all the might-have-beens coming together in a final thunderclap of transformation ... all my ideas returning to air ...

There is only one small thing I know to be true ... hope and meaning rise with the sun every morning ... there has never been a better time to be alive ... something huge is happening just outside the frame of my thinking ...

[SOUND: *baby cooing.*]

[LIGHTS *fade slowly on Trent. A sense that he is the baby floating in black space.*]

[CURTAIN CALL: *'Walk Away, Renee'.*]

[Audience recessional: Al Green, 'Love and Happiness'.]

END

AUTHOR'S ACKNOWLEDGEMENTS

Thanks to the actors who participated in the development of this play: Peter Donaldson, Todd Duckworth, Victor Ertmanis, Megan Follows, Deborah Hay, Shannon Lawson, Richard McMillan, Susan Monis, Eric Peterson, Linda Prystawska, Paul Rainville, Julian Ritchings, Waneta Storms and R.H. Thomson.

Thanks also to Ken Gass (Factory Theatre), Marti Maraden (NAC) and Don Shipley (Harbourfront World Stage) for their faith in the project.

Special thanks to friends who read various drafts of the play and provided timely advice: Richard Addis, Margaret Atwood, Russell Banks, David Cole, Ludwig Max Fischer, Robert Fones, Brian Freeman, Linda Griffiths, Marni Jackson, Linda McQuaig, Michael Ondaatje, Tony Penikett, Brian Rodgers, His Excellency John Ralston Saul and Helen Schlesinger. Special thanks to Ronald Wright for the Mayan riffs that inspired Trent's last day.

Over the years George and Martha Butterfield have provided vital financial support for Necessary Angel: blessings upon them. Thanks also to Scott Griffin and Michael Young for their financial help with the premiere production of this play.

ABOUT THE AUTHOR

DAVID YOUNG is best known for his plays *Glenn* (Stratford Festival, 1999) and *Inexpressible Island*. His other plays (with Paul LeDoux) include *Fire* and *Love Is Strange*. David is the author of two novels and has written extensively for radio, television and film. In a former life he was President of the Coach House Press for ten years.

Typeset in Cartier Book
at Coach House Printing on bpNichol Lane, 2001

Edited and designed by damian lopes, Alana Wilcox and
Darren Wershler-Henry

Address production inquiries to:
dsy@sympatico.ca

To read the online version of this text and other titles from
Coach House Books, visit our website:
www.chbooks.com

To add your name to our e-mailing list, write:
mail@chbooks.com

Toll-free:
1 800 376 6360

Coach House Books
401 Huron Street on bpNichol Lane
Toronto, Ontario
M5S 2G5